THE
POCKET
CHEERLEADER

THE POCKET CHEERLEADER

BANGS CAREY-CAMPBELL

unbound

First published in 2020

Unbound
6th Floor Mutual House, 70 Conduit Street, London W1S 2GF
www.unbound.com

Text Design by PDQ Digital Media Solutions

Illustrations © Nadezda_Grapes

A CIP record for this book is available from the British Library

ISBN 978-1-78352-754-0 (paperback)
ISBN 978-1-78352-755-7 (ebook)

Printed in Great Britain by CPI Group (UK)

1 3 5 7 9 8 6 4 2

For Mama, Papa and Our Kid – the best cheerleaders a girl could ever ask for.

And for Mikey – I wish I'd have cheered for you more.

Contents

For Your Spirit

Premium Pep Talks

Introduction

Welcome to *The Pocket Cheerleader: Your Badass Guide to Getting Moving* – a little pocket cheerleader that'll give you that kick up the ass on the days you can't remember why you set your alarm so damn early for that [insert whichever workout you currently want to erase from your life] class.

Fitness has hit the big time over the past few years. We all know we should be doing it, we get the general concept: health benefits, yada yada yada, yeah yeah, we know. But that doesn't actually change the reality that, some days, it can just be really frikkin' hard to get your ass in gear and go do it.

So many people are still carrying around the trauma of high-school PE lessons. When you think about it, it's not surprising. At a time in our lives where we're feeling the most vulnerable about our bodies, we're made to get changed in front of other people and don ill-fitting shorts and T-shirts. If you were late to class, you'd be forced to run laps (hardly the way to make good associations with being active) and if you were playing a team sport and you sucked, well, then you had a herd of rowdy teenagers ridiculing you. Oh, the joy!

But we're adults now, with the power of choice. We don't have to let the pain of not being picked as goal attack for the high-school netball team dictate the way our fitness should go for the rest of our lives (and we don't have to borrow kit from the lost-property box *shudders*). Still, making the decision to commit to getting and staying fit is a hard one.

How do I know this? Well, I spent many a year as a champion couch potato. I was a dancer when I was younger, but once I graduated from university and went off to live in different countries, physical activity just slipped further and further down my list of priorities until it wasn't one at all.

The height of my inactivity came when I was living in Toronto. It's not a coincidence that I was also feeling very low at the time: isolated, unfocused, mentally and emotionally drained, completely drifting with regards to my career goals and no clue how to get my life back on track.

I returned to the UK and moved in with my parents while I figured things out – not exactly where I imagined myself being at twenty-nine. There was no structure or focus in my life at the time and I just felt very… 'blah'.

I thought back to my dancer days and remembered how good it felt to just move. At this point, I was getting winded simply walking up a flight of stairs. I needed something to help me get fitter. I've always enjoyed watching boxing, and someone told me that was a great way to boost your cardio, so I thought I'd give it a try.

I hadn't worked out in years at this point, but I took a chance and walked into a down-and-dirty boxing gym in Leeds. To say it was 'no frills' would be an understatement. The stench of sweat hit you as you ascended the stairs and the equipment was in tatters. The class had about twenty-five guys and three women (one of whom owned the gym). It was a little intimidating.

For an hour and a half we did sit-ups, press-ups, burpees, star jumps, and round upon round of punching a heavy bag. By the end of it, I couldn't remember my own name, I could barely lift my arms and practically needed someone to give me a piggyback out of there. But I was ecstatic.

Adrenalin and endorphins pumped around my body – I was absolutely giddy. It had been such a hard session, but I wanted to get straight back in there and do it all over again. I felt kinda cheated – why had no one told me that throwing myself around and getting sweaty could make me feel *this* good? Exercise for women, according to the media, should be all about how we look, but why wasn't anyone talking about this *feeling*? While I was annoyed I hadn't found it sooner, I was SOLD! I was all in!

That boxing class became like a religion to me. Every Thursday night I'd be there. It gave me something to look forward to; it was the one bit of structure I had in my life. Week after week I found my skills improving, but not only that, I was walking taller, I felt more confident, had a sense of purpose, a spring in my step. That class turned my life around.

So, I've been committed to the sweat life since '09. I'm now a spin instructor and fitness editor, so if there's one thing I'm pretty good at, it's motivating myself and others to push through in the moments you'd rather be doing anything else.

One thing fitness has given me is the ability to be an utter badass in every area of my life. It's taught me perseverance, determination, mindfulness, focus, how to love and respect my body. Those are the things that helped make fitness a habit for me. So, if you're looking for the key to rock-hard abs and slimmer thighs, you came to the wrong place. You'll see no reference to that here. I'm not of the belief that a six-pack will make your life better. But a commitment to getting sweaty pretty regularly will.

You will have days when you don't want to do it, you've had enough, your spirit is broken, you feel uninspired or you're just bored of it all. That's natural: it happens to everyone and it's not a reason to give up. This book is here to help get you through those moments and remind you why you started this journey into sweat to begin with.

The meteoric rise of all things fitness-related over recent years has brought with it an overcomplication of something that should be a fun, enjoyable, stress-relieving part of your daily routine. It's time to strip things back, simplify it all and get back to learning to love simply moving more and staying motivated to do it.

The current fitness scene can make it seem like the only reason to set foot in a gym is to take a selfie in the mirror, or get a little fitter so you can do more gym classes. But what about the everyday practicalities of life that fitness can help you with? It'd be kinda nice to be able to break out into a run for the bus without feeling like you need a quadruple bypass, right? To bend down to pick something up off the floor without throwing your back out? Or not be filled with dread when your boss suggests doing a 5k run for charity as a team-building exercise?

We tend to forget that exercise doesn't necessarily mean three-hour gym sessions, pushing ourselves to the very brink. Simply put, staying active makes movement easier. And while we might like to think of ourselves as Peter Pan, the reality is that we're all getting older. So, doing squats? They'll help you be able to sit down and stand up with ease. Shoulder presses? You'll be able to lift something heavy onto a shelf at home. An occasional run? Keeps your ticker healthy.

Exercise doesn't have to be all about six-pack abs and glistening muscles in Instagram shots. Moving more just makes the inner workings of your life easier – it's as simple as that, really.

4

So, in this here book, you'll find sixty short chapters, conveniently split into these six subsections so you can dip in where you need to and get maximum motivational bang for your buck that day.

Get Going

Whether you're just starting out in fitness or aiming to make a triumphant return to the gym after a period of 'can't be arsed-ness', the 'Get Going' chapters equip you with the basics. Everything you need to get you in the game, from the right playlist to the best frame of mind in which to approach your workouts.

Inspiration Station

Need some ideas on how to keep your workout life interesting? The last thing we want is for exercise to feel like a chore, so these chapters will help you mix it up. Keeping it creative and different helps you stay engaged in the process.

Mind Over Matter

The importance of a strong mental attitude in fitness is often brushed aside to focus on the physical. These chapters are for those moments when you need to remind yourself of the bigger picture and find that inner strength to push you through the days when you want to quit.

If You're Flagging...

So maybe you've been working out for a while now. It was going great, but you've hit a roadblock. We all have moments where we feel unmotivated – these chapters will hold your hand and guide you back to the supreme level of badassery you almost very nearly strayed from by giving you simple, handy hacks to jump-start you back into the game.

For Your Spirit

Oh, you thought fitness was just about your body? Ha! Have a gander at these chapters when you need to connect the dots between that elevated heart rate and the burning desire for a better you in your soul.

Premium Pep Talks

When you've tried every which way to talk yourself out of a workout, flip to these chapters and slap some sense into yourself (physically slapping yourself with the book is optional, though not recommended).

Before you get going, invest in some good quality kit. Familiarise yourself with some super-sexy Lycra – a nice pair of leggings or shorts, a breathable vest top. Areas it's always a good idea to pay extra attention to are your boobs and your feet. Ladies, for the love of God, invest in a good sports bra. No – wearing two normal underwired bras on top of each other does not a sports bra make. In all seriousness, not having the proper support in that area can cause damage to your fun bags, and no one wants that.

For your feet, go to a reputable sports store and speak to one of the assistants there about your needs. Will you be wearing these trainers mainly in the gym? Or do you think running might be more your thing? If it's running, they'll do what they call a 'gait analysis' by putting you on a treadmill, seeing how you run and getting you in a pair of trainers that will support your feet properly. It's worth doing this to save yourself time, energy and blisters down the line.

So, dive in. A healthier relationship with exercise, your body, mind and the way you move through life awaits you on the other side.

Get Going

1. Set a goal

I know some people still work out to lose weight, but at this point we know there's a whole bunch more to this fitness thing than that, and really there *has* to be. Even if that is your primary goal, sooner or later you've got to find some other reasons, otherwise what happens when you lose the weight? You just stop?

Also, it's worth pausing for a second to really analyse why it is that you think you need to lose weight. We are constantly bombarded with images of an 'ideal' body type, but who decided that was the ideal? There are plenty of people who don't fit into that very narrow template, yet they're still considered very attractive and they're out there living their best lives. So, if weight loss is your ultimate fitness goal, first I want you to take a moment to really delve into why that's so important to you. What do you think will happen? You'll lose 10 lbs and suddenly you'll be the person who brokers an international peace deal?

Alternatively, you could work out to become mentally stronger, so that you can resist the constant barrage of bullshit that makes you feel you're not good enough to begin with.

So, let's think bigger picture here. Rather than anything to do with losing weight, let's think of the goal as something we can *gain*, something that zones in on boosting our ability. Whether it's to run a half-marathon, lift a certain amount in your deadlifts or do twenty push-ups non-stop, make it about something that's going to make you stronger, more determined and focused. Take the focus off the aesthetics of your body and set a goal around what's going to motivate you on a deeper level.

Tip: Don't just think it up willy-nilly – write it down. When you see it in ink, on paper, it serves as a reminder. It's more purposeful; it's a commitment. And also, let's be real, it's an excuse to buy nice stationery.

Mantra: I'm working towards a better me in mind, body and soul.

2. Make the most super-awesome shape-throwing playlist known to humankind

Ahh, one of the most important parts of any fitness journey: the music. You only need to forget your headphones once to know you never want to suffer through your gym's atrocious musical taste ever again. Music is a massive motivator. On days when it can be tough to find a reason to train, throwing on some tunes that are guaranteed to get you moving is a pretty fail-safe way to ensure you get out there and get it done.

The making of a good workout playlist is a fine art. You don't wanna just go in there, guns blazing, with a ton of big, heavy tracks. Let your playlist take you on a journey. Include songs that make you feel strong and powerful, songs that bring back happy memories or have gotten you through tough times.

There are no hard and fast rules – go with what works for you. Be open to different musical genres. Hell, there might be a particular operatic aria that makes you feel like an utter badass while you lift some heavy weights. Whatever floats your boat.

Your playlist may well vary based on the type of workout you're doing. Chilled-out yoga session? Going for music with a slower tempo will encourage you to slow down and focus on your movement and technique. Busting out a high-powered HIIT session? Big beats, massive drops, music that's sonically large will help you feel energised throughout.

Think of the way your workout will be structured too. Ease in with some light-hearted tunes for your warm-up, throw in something with a bit more kick in it as you up your speed on the treadmill. Get some big bangers in there for when you hit the weights – opting for something with lyrics that push you always helps. Then throttle back, perhaps with a little neo-soul, for your cool-down and stretch.

Jay-Z may never know that I rap *The Blueprint* album in its entirety at least once a week while I work out, but I'm pretty sure it's a scientific fact that I am 100 per cent more badass by the end of those sessions. Tina Turner's 'Proud Mary' has gotten me through the final push of many a workout, Morcheeba has soundtracked most of my Pilates classes, and for when I really need to cut loose, big dance remixes of Rihanna classics never fail.

Tip: Ask friends for input – get them to send you songs that remind them of you or fun times you've had together.

Mantra: This is my playlist of power!

3. Schedule your workout like a business meeting

One of our main excuses for not working out is that we don't have time. We'll somehow manage to squeeze a ton of other things into our day, not all of which are essential, but the one thing that really is important, which can have an impact on the way we conduct every aspect of our day, that we'll happily forgo.

Literally write your workout time in your day planner, block that time out and let nothing interfere with it. Your workout should be sacred. There are plenty of things you can flake out on in life – after-work boozing (you always regret that the next day), that panel discussion you got tickets for ages ago but don't give a crap about now, your partner's boss's leaving party – all totally flakable. Your workout, however: no. Stop giving yourself an easy out. Stop letting it be the first thing you cancel when your day gets a bit swamped.

Your workout isn't a luxury. It's a necessity. When you work out, your brain functions better, you're more focused and on point, and surely everyone around you wins when you're like that, right? Right. You're the boss of your body. Stop accepting late notes from your brain.

Tip: Keep some spare workout kit at your office so you can never use the excuse that you don't have kit with you.

Mantra: Barack Obama made time to work out when he was the leader of the free world. If he can squeeze it in, so can you.

4. Keep a log

After every workout, when you're in that blissful, post-sweat endorphin haze, write down how you feel. On days when you're lacking motivation, having a journal of sorts to look back on can be a great reminder about the potential high that awaits on the other side of a sweat-fest. Write whatever words come to mind: empowered, strong, sweaty, exhausted, happy, peaceful, buzzin'!

If there were songs used in the workout that you really vibed to, make a note of them. Particular exercises that you really liked? Whack those down in there too. Anything that'll help you remember everything about that workout that made you feel on top of the world, scribble it in your book. When you're searching for motivation, you can read through it and recreate the components in your head. It'll conjure up all those feelings and you'll be throwing on fresh Lycra and heading out the door before you know it.

Tip: Make this part of your workout ritual. Work out, grab a bite to eat after, and perhaps while you're enjoying a post-sweat green tea you take the time to jot down your workout notes.

Mantra: 'We are what we repeatedly do. Excellence, then, is not an act, but a habit.' – Will Durant

5. The ten-minute rule

As much as you may love your workouts, there'll be days when you won't. There'll be days when you just can't be arsed. However hard you try, sometimes there are sweat sessions that you just dread or can't get into.

Shameless name-drop moment, but I once interviewed Paula Radcliffe. She has held the women's marathon world record for fifteen solid years, so she knows a thing or two about running. I asked her what she did on days where she just couldn't get into it or a run was going terribly. She introduced me to her 'ten-minute rule' technique. Start your workout and if after ten minutes you're still feeling completely crappy and just can't get your head in the game, call it a day, go home and chill out.

Sometimes you'll find all you need is to get started and you can find your groove – after those first ten minutes, you've found your stride and you're feeling better. But if it goes the other way, just chalk it up to it being a crappy day and move on. Don't beat yourself up about it; don't dwell on it. Tomorrow's a new day and another opportunity to kick ass.

Tip: If you're just feeling generally out of sorts but a workout is a bridge too far for you today, try to get outside and have a stroll. Some time outside and fresh air can make the world of difference.

Mantra: 'If at first you don't succeed, you are running about average.' – M. H. Alderson

6. Set yourself mini-challenges

Constantly thinking of your overall goal can be a pretty heavy load to bear. If you don't feel you're moving towards it quickly enough, it can turn into a slippery slope of discouragement pretty fast. Sometimes the bigger picture is just way too overwhelming and pretty scary to look at.

So, you've gotta break that bad boy down. If you're in marathon training and the prospect of running ten miles makes you want to jump down the nearest pothole, break it down. You just need to tackle it a mile at a time. Plan your route so that you'll see something interesting at every three-mile mark and reward yourself by stopping and taking a picture, texting a friend or having a dance break. I've done runs where I had to break it down from lamp post to lamp post, tree to parking meter, postbox to dustbin – whatever helps you to reframe that moment and stop those feelings from overwhelming you, USE IT.

We're living in times where we want everything yesterday. But progress takes patience. You won't magically wake up one day with the physical ability of your favourite superhero. It takes time. You just need to keep showing up for yourself. Little by little, you get there.

Tip: Burpees are my nemesis. If I'm in a class and they say to do as many burpees as you can in thirty seconds and I'm feeling like my entire soul has left my body after doing six of them, I set myself the mini-challenge of trying to hit ten. I don't worry about everyone around me zipping through them, I just charge on with my own personal battle and still feel a sense of achievement if I get ten in the bag.

Mantra: Even if they're baby steps, I'm still moving forward.

7. Focus on the feeling

Better than any drug you can get on the street, endorphins are free and you just need to get a bit sweaty to experience them. That feeling at the end of your workout when you're exhausted, giddy, discombobulated and ecstatic all at once, feeling like you could either take on the world or have a hard nap at any given moment – those are endorphins working their wonderful magic.

But when we think of working out, we tend to focus on the struggle of it, how hard it's gonna be, whether we'll be able to keep up. Will I be embarrassed if I don't get it? What if everyone else there is better than me?

On top of this add pretty much everything that's pushed at us fitness-wise about how we should change our bodies. How to get a flatter stomach now, a thigh gap tomorrow, a six-pack in a week, a Kardashian ass in a month. When we're starting from the viewpoint that we have something wrong that needs to change, the prospect of changing it isn't exactly going to be fun: 'I don't fit into this body ideal, so I *have* to do this to be accepted.'

Repeat after me: BOLLOCKS!

This isn't about trying to mould and shape your body a certain way. We didn't create these body ideals, so why are we succumbing to the pressure to conform to them? This is about *feeling* good. It's about seeing something through, being determined, focused, confident and reaping the rewards of that.

And that's what you should chase. Not a six-pack or faster race times, just simply that feeling of achievement rushing around your body, firing happy signals into your brain, reminding you that it was worth it as you drip with sweat and get your breath back.

Let yourself feel that feeling. Breathe heavy, let that smile spread across your face, skip through the car park, high-five that stranger – this is your moment of glory. Endorphins are the reward.

Chase that feeling.

Tip: Refer back to Chapter 4 – remember that logbook that you're diligently keeping of all your workouts? This is a good time to refer back to it, to remind yourself how those workouts made you feel.

Mantra: Sweaty euphoria is hella sexy!

8. Surround yourself with people who celebrate you

Everyone has goals and dreams, and while a lot of people like to refer to themselves as 'self-made', you've gotta have people in your corner who will cheer you on. You need people who'll celebrate your victories with you, be interested in your quest, give you that boost when you need it and, overall, want you to succeed. Staying focused and driven is hard. Having people who will pick you up when you stumble and listen to you when you grumble is essential.

So those people who give you those subtle jabs – you know the ones: mocking you when you opt out of going to the pub or you leave somewhere early in favour of going for a workout – yeah, those aren't your people. It may all seem innocent enough but, on some level, they just don't want to see you succeed. If they see you trying to make a change in your life, doing something that makes you happy, more confident, more focused, and they're your friend, they should be showing an interest in it and offering their support. If they're not doing that, it's OK to distance yourself from them a little.

To stay on the right path in your workout life, you need support and encouragement – there are plenty of people out there willing to give you that.

Find your tribe.

Tip: Be sure that you're that person for someone else too, so you understand how powerful it can be.

Mantra: We're stronger together.

9. Let your workout set the tone for how you live your life

The great thing about fitness is that it can give you very literal metaphors for life. You can zone in and make it purely about pushing your body and doing the best you can during that session, or you can take it further and let your approach to that workout be symbolic of how you want your day to go.

Are you going to quit as soon as the going gets tough in your day? Are you going to cut corners and make excuses? Are you going to search for the easy way out? Pah! Of course not! You regroup, try a different approach, take a breather and come back to it with fresh energy, but you don't just throw in the towel the second something seems undoable. Every bicep curl, crow pose, plank or push-up is an opportunity to recommit to the focus, dedication and determination you want to have in the other areas of your life. When you do think of it on that deeper level, it makes you that much more committed and gives each moment of sweat that little bit more meaning. Let this newfound steely determination you've discovered in your workouts permeate through every aspect of your life.

If you wouldn't quit in the middle of a meeting at work, don't give in midway through some kettlebell swings. Grit your teeth, dig deeper and dream bigger.

Tip: Take a few moments before your workout. Close your eyes, take some deep breaths and think of how you want to feel during your day, be it powerful, assertive, productive, balanced … Just taking a few seconds to remind yourself of what you truly want will help you develop a more focused approach to your workout.

Mantra: I will not give up on me.

10. Listen to your body

If there's one thing exercise will do, it'll make you appreciate your body. You get so in tune with it and learn to respect it as the finely oiled machine that it is. Once you get hooked on exercise, be it the endorphin high, the routine of it, that crazy-hot instructor you're always trying to impress (I don't judge), it can be hard sometimes to forgo that feeling. You can end up pushing your body to the brink. You'll try to ignore that little niggle in your knee, or that tightness in your hamstring and soldier on regardless.

But pushing through an injury doesn't make you a martyr – it just makes you a bit daft. When your body is grumbling in the form of pulled muscles, tightness, soreness or just sheer exhaustion, do yourself – and everyone else around you – a favour and listen to it. Take some rest. Go and see a physio. Take care of yourself. Continuing to work out while injured will only make it worse. Get some treatment for whatever the issue is, take the required recovery time and come back stronger.

Your hard work won't all go to crap if you sit out a couple of sessions. Managing an injury will make you appreciate your body that much more.

Tip: The key is in prevention. Taking the time to warm up properly pre-workout and then a few minutes afterwards to stretch will make the world of difference. People love to skip the stretch portion of a workout at the end, then wonder why their muscles are tight or they're always getting injured. Don't be that person.

Mantra: I refuse to beat myself up.

Inspiration Station

11. Find what you love - and do more of it

Your workout should never be a punishment or a chore. You shouldn't loathe it, dread it or hide from it. If you feel any of those things right now, your current workout regime simply ain't for you. That doesn't mean fitness isn't your thing (you're not getting out of it that easily!), it just means you haven't found the right fit yet.

We need to abandon this notion that if it isn't a 10k run or three-hour gym session, it doesn't count. Bollocks. As long as you're moving, you're making a steady payment into the bank of body-movement badassery. Experiment, live a little, find what works for you. Maybe it's parkour or a Beyoncé dance class, rollerblading or t'ai chi – the possibilities are endless. Find the thing that gets you moving and makes you happy and you'll find the rest just slots into place like the finest of jigsaw puzzles.

It can take a while to find that thing, but don't get frustrated in your pursuit of it. It's all part of the process. Everyone's journey is different. What works for one person (an exercise routine that challenges them, makes them happy, has them sprinkling endorphins everywhere like glitter and inhabiting a zone of supreme badassery) may not work for you. And when you find your 'thing', it might not work for someone else. There's no 'right' way to go about fitness. However you choose to move, in whatever way makes you happy, consider that the ideal way for you. That may well change from week to week or month to month, but the best part is the pursuit of finding those things that give you that buzz.

I've been through many phases since I started my fitness journey – boxing, running, dance classes, rollerskating (which I'm terrible at, but makes me smile ear to ear nonetheless), Pilates, spinning, HIIT classes, weight training, trampolining – you name it, I've given it a go.

As much as I'd like to be one of those people on Instagram who strikes bold yoga poses on white sandy beaches, every yoga class I've ever been to has bored me almost to actual tears. I'm not going to beat myself up for not liking it. It just ain't for me. I tried it; I don't like it. NEXT!

I often have people asking me for advice about getting into running. They'll tell me, 'I've tried it, but I just can't get into it. I don't enjoy it. What am I doing wrong?' Listen, we all have busy lives – why are you going to waste time doing something you don't enjoy? Running isn't compulsory. This isn't school. You don't *have* to do it. If you've tried it and you don't like it, don't do it. Simples. Just keep trying activities 'til something sticks and you find yourself saying, 'I definitely don't wanna miss that session next week.' Then you're on to a winner.

Tip: Don't box yourself in to certain types of workouts and completely write other ones off. You never know – you might think you hate swimming, but after giving it a go, you may find that that's the thing that brings you the most satisfaction. Stay open to the possibilities.

Mantra: If it makes me smile, I'm doing it!

12. Bribe yourself

You know when you were a kid and your mum used to say that if you behaved yourself while you were out shopping with her, she'd get you a treat? And you acted like a child sent directly from heaven, based purely on the promise of a Cadbury's Creme Egg? You know why your mum did that? 'Cause bribery works! And while I'm sure we'd all like to think we're above it now as adults, we're pretty much wired the same way.

So, whatever your challenge is, pick out something you'll reward yourself with at the end of it. Maybe it's if you do three months of a particular kind of workout you go on holiday, or get those shoes you've wanted for ages, or a nice dinner at your favourite restaurant – whatever turns you on. But let it be the carrot on a stick until you complete your mission.

Tip: Don't make it something so financially grandiose that you can't afford it when you hit your goal – no one needs that kind of let-down!

Mantra: Good things come to those who sweat.

13. Friends who sweat together stay together

Sometimes, going for that run by yourself is super-boring, or it's really intimidating to go to a new class for the first time alone. This is why you need a fitness buddy, a ride-or-die friend who's down to Lycra up and get as sweaty as can be whenever the workout gods call.

For friends Kim Ngo, Rachel Tran and Laura Lakam, working out together is a core part of their friendship. They even founded a website, Food & Lycra (www.foodandlycra. com), to document their sweaty adventures.

It began with running. Laura had started pounding the pavements and persuaded the other girls to join her. 'We were all friends, beginners and on the same journey,' says Rachel. 'So it just made sense for us to do it together.'

So just how important is it that they make time to exercise with each other? 'Very, very important,' Rachel continues. 'We're each other's motivators and hype men. We encourage, but we also congratulate, be it big or small successes.'

'Our group workouts have improved my motivation,' says Laura. 'It's so easy to give up when you're on your own. You have no one to give you that little push. When you work out in a group, you just get encouraged. If I feel like stopping or giving up, there's always someone to give me a friendly reminder that I need to keep on moving.'

'When I work out on my own, it's refocus and hustle time,' says Kim, who's a PT, so tends to lead the workouts with her Food & Lycra crew. 'When I'm with the girls, it's less about that; it's more a reminder that this is still fun and we have a solid group of women who are shouting "YAAASSSS!" to all our achievements.'

I know what you're thinking: 'This sounds great, but all

my friends hate exercise.' So, how do you go about finding yourself a workout buddy when you're surrounded by people who may not exactly be willing volunteers? 'Try and convince your friends or your family to go and do a class with you or go for a run. If your friends are anything like mine, you might need to bribe them with food, so have some kind of reward at the end, like brunch or dinner. Trust me, it works!' says Kim.

'If they're super-stubborn, try and go to classes alone. You would be surprised who you can meet in a class. I have so many regulars at my classes, some of them have become friends, BFFs and some maybe a bit more! By being at your favourite class, you've already got something in common and it could be the start of a lovely (and sweaty) friendship!'

Staying motivated can be hard, so it just helps to have someone around who gets you. They'll understand your endorphin high, your hatred of whichever sadist invented burpees, your meltdowns when you think there's absolutely no way in Idris Elba's (i.e. God's) green earth you can do one more press-up, 'cause they're right there feeling that struggle with you. You can motivate and encourage each other, get a bit of friendly competition going on. There is no workout you can't conquer when you take it on together.

Tip: Schedule the days you'll work out together for a month, get them down in your diary and commit to them. You're less likely to flake when you know you'll be letting someone down.

Mantra: Friendships grow stronger when bonded by sweat.

14. Variety is the spice of life

You may well have found a workout that you like and want to just cherish that and do it for ever and ever, and that's great, but variety is the spice of life, my friend. Clocking endless miles and never doing any strength training isn't a great idea, nor is spending all your time in the weights section and doing no cardio.

Put it this way: what good is it being able to run for (and never miss) the bus, but not being able to carry a bag of heavy groceries more than a few metres? Or being able to lift all the heavy things, having a super-buff and toned physique, but the day the zombie apocalypse comes, you can't outrun any of those mofos?

Switch your workouts up, not only to keep it interesting for you, but to challenge your body in different ways. It needs that. If you want to see changes in your abilities, you've got to keep your body guessing and make it work for it.

Tip: If you know you're a total boss when it comes to HIIT workouts, this gives you a chance to strengthen skills you might neglect – doing a Pilates class to work on your core strength, for example.

Mantra: 'Sameness is the mother of disgust, variety the cure.' – Petrarch

15. Create a fit environment

If you want to maintain a fit lifestyle, it's probably best not to set up camp in a pub, stock your fridge with the worst foods or conduct your entire life from a beanbag.

Build your life in a way that's going to help you succeed. At work, ditch the office chair for a fitness ball, so that every day, without realising it, you're building core strength and better posture. Space things around the office so you have to get up and walk to reach them.

At home, make a point of keeping filtered water in your fridge, not having unhealthy snacks around and maybe keeping a yoga mat in sight to remind you to stretch.

Keep constant little reminders around 'til it's just the way you lead your life and you don't even think about it.

Tip: Set an alarm for yourself so that every thirty minutes you have to get up from your desk and move a little.

Mantra: Healthy mind, healthy home, healthy life.

16. Take the stairs

Take the stairs not just because it's another way to build movement into your day, or because taking a lift to go two floors when you're perfectly capable of walking does indeed make you a lazy bugger. Do it because it's a good metaphor. By taking the stairs, you're not taking the easy option. It'll take you longer, it's more effort, it's not always convenient.

And, sometimes, that's the way fitness and your training can go. Sometimes it pays to slow down, take the long route, let things be a little harder, in order to understand the importance of the process. Taking the stairs builds a good foundation. It's a reminder that although shortcuts are quicker, you might miss the lesson.

Tip: Use it as an opportunity to see how your fitness is improving. At the beginning of the month, time how long it takes you to get up those few flights of stairs. Then time yourself again at the end of the month, so you can revel in how badass you're becoming.

Mantra: There's no elevator to success.

17. Try something new

People are often scared to branch out of what they know for fear of looking a little silly if they don't get the hang of something straight away. We've already covered how variety is the spice of life (and your workouts). When things get a little stagnant and you need to inject a bit of something to fire you up again, throw yourself a curveball.

Maybe rock climbing, pole dancing, circus skills, aerial yoga – try something out of left field, something you'd never usually do, that'll require you to use your body in a different way. It'll give you a new challenge, break up your routine, maybe even give you a new workout to add to your regular ones. That newness can shake things up, change your perspective and get you excited about your body again.

Trying something new is going to throw you off your game somewhat, and if we're sticking with the 'Let your workout set the tone for how you live your life' idea (Chapter 9), you need that every now and then. When we get really good at something, it's hard to try something new and have to be the novice, unsure of how things work and battling with the fact that your ability might not be as good in that area.

But this happens in life too.

What if life serves you some major lemons and you lose your job, and your next job is quite a departure from your last role, with an abundance of new things to learn? Where do you get the confidence to know that you'll weather that storm?

Well, you can just remind yourself of that time you tried a new workout and sucked at it at first, but kept at it and saw gradual improvements every week. *That's* where!

Tip: Drag a friend along to make the whole thing less intimidating.

Mantra: Nothing ventured, nothing gained.

18. Follow like-minded people on social media

If you're the only person in your immediate circle who is all about this fitness life, it can be pretty hard. If you're slaying it at a HIIT class while all your mates are down the pub, it's easy to lose motivation. A kick-ass support network is essential to keep you on the right track.

Take today to go through all your social media accounts and follow people who truly motivate and inspire you. You might like their message, or their exercise demos, or perhaps they put up challenges that you like to have a go at. Curate your feeds with things you find uplifting, which give you a boost and make you want to move.

When you check your phone first thing in the morning (which is a bad habit, by the way – you should stop doing that), seeing an Instagram feed of fit, happy people enjoying their workout is a surefire way to make you jump out of bed and get to it.

Tip: Equally, if there are people on your social media feeds who make you feel negative about your body or the way you're living your life, utilise that unfollow or block button.

Mantra: I will keep my worldview positive and focused.

19. Do it for the 'Gram

If you've lost sight of all the reasons why you should exercise today and are in the middle of building a blanket fort on your couch, let me offer you this nugget: go somewhere different to do your workout and make it your mission to take an interesting picture for Instagram.

Sure, there's plenty to mock about the trend of the 'pics or it didn't happen' workout culture and I'm not suggesting here that you document every moment of your sweat life. We don't need to see every bicep curl, squat and pigeon pose. But combining your creativity with your workouts can lead to some interesting content and gives you something to look back at that will motivate you on the days where you struggle. It's a good way to track your journey.

Get up super-early for a run, specifically so you can capture the sunrise. Or grab your fitness buddy, go to a part of town you've never been to, do a HIIT workout and take a pic of a particularly supafly building or landmark. It gives your regular workout a bit of a twist, a new goal to throw in with the rest, something else to focus on – and you can get creative with it.

Plus, anything is a step up from the standard gym-mirror selfie, amirite?

Tip: When I go on runs and see something interesting, I'll sit on the ground, stretch my legs out in front of me and take a picture of my trainers with said interesting thing in the background. Looking at those pics reminds me of all the cool places these feet have taken me.

Mantra: I can work out and win a photography prize too!

20. Make it a social occasion

Gone are the days when you worked out in your living room to a Jane Fonda video, wearing an old T-shirt you used to decorate in, before going off to work. You're allowed to be seen out in your Lycra now. Dishevelled and sweaty is the new black.

If you know there's a workout that's particularly tough, you've been scared to try or you just can't get motivated to do, make it a social occasion. Book spots in the class for you and a few friends, then go to brunch or dinner after. Tying it to something bigger than the workout itself means you're less likely to flake out, and you won't want to let your friends down (but more importantly, if there's food involved, it'd just be rude to not partake in that).

A 2016 Dove study showed only 20 per cent of UK women describe themselves as body confident. Why does that matter? Because nine out of ten women opt out of important life activities, such as engaging with friends and loved ones or doing some exercise, when they don't feel good about their bodies.

So by making your workouts a more social occasion, you're ticking positive boxes. Sure, it's great that you're working out, but you might also be giving a friend with low self-esteem the confidence boost she was looking for, or helping an introverted friend get social and not feel awkward. Working out together normalises getting sweaty and is a great way to bring an overall sense of wellbeing to yourself and those around you.

Tip: Wear your best/fanciest Lycra.

Mantra: Post-workout brunch is the new post-club kebab.

Mind Over Matter

21. Get comfortable being uncomfortable

It's all too easy to stay in that zone in your workout where it's *just* challenging enough, where it's an effort, but it's not killing you. You're just a couple of steps above phoning it in, really. You're doing what you're capable of. But to really dig deep, to really get to the guts of this thing, to tap into what's going to make you stronger not only in body but in mind, you have to be willing to take it to the ugly and get uncomfortable.

You're holding back out of fear. You're not sure what happens when you colour outside those lines. You're not sure if you're going to be able to do it, so rather than risk the embarrassment of failure, you're willing to not try.

Camilla Henderson, a sport and exercise performance consultant who has worked with professionals in the worlds of football, rugby, horse riding, swimming and more, knows what it takes to tap into that part of your brain that can take you further.

'Before diving into getting uncomfortable, we have to have high levels of self-efficacy [a belief in your ability to achieve goals], self-worth and self-esteem,' she says. All of those things take time and patience to develop. So to help you get there, 'Think about the things you do well, that you're really good at, the kinds of things you find comfortable and easy,' says Camilla. 'What are you good at? Think to yourself, "When in the past have I done really well? When have I been really happy and felt a great sense of achievement?" Use those past experiences, where you've felt positive, and take those processes with you to bolster yourself in that moment before a challenge.'

Camilla also stresses the importance of our mindset and how that determines our behaviours. Our own self-talk and thought processes can often set the agenda for our actions that day. If your internal dialogue is: 'I feel crappy today. Nothing ever works out for me. This training session is going to be terrible!', it doesn't take a genius to figure out where that will lead you once you hit the gym floor.

We want to create more autonomy over our thought processes, particularly the negative ones. Camilla advises her clients to commit to more positive thoughts, to be really self-aware and more reflective. 'Have conversations with friends and family about the goals you're setting for yourself,' she says. Talk about why you want to do it, why it's important to you and the steps you're taking to get there. Having that kind of chatter regularly will get you feeling more positive about the task at hand. 'The process is always more important than the outcome,' says Camilla. 'View your challenges as an opportunity, rather than, "Oh my God, what can go wrong here?" Your perception of the challenge is so important.'

The thought of getting into an uncomfortable zone can be overwhelming. Before they take that leap, Camilla will often ask her clients to write two lists: things they're in control of and things they aren't in control of. The key is to ensure the 'in control' list is longer. 'Things you're in control of might be: your thought process, getting yourself ready, getting there on time, warming yourself up. Things you're not in control of could be: the number of people there, the specific exercises they're doing in the class, maybe the music that's playing. You might not always like what's on either list, but ask yourself to respond to anything on the uncontrollable list with a positive action or statement that brings control back to you.'

In weighing up all those factors and committing to more positive self-talk, it's also important that you set the agenda for your session based on how you feel that day. 'Do a self-assessment,' Camilla advises. 'Did I get enough sleep? How's my body feeling? Did I eat enough today? Your expectations should be based on truth, fact and reality.'

Any gains worth having in life come from taking the risk. Today, step up to your fear, don't back down from the fight, be willing to get uncomfortable and show yourself that what you've been saying is your limit is very far from it.

Anyone you look up to or admire in life who is pushing limits in their field did not get there by playing it safe.

So mentally prepare yourself for what happens when you take the leap and push further; imagine how much harder your heart will beat, feel your breathlessness, accept that your arms, legs, core (anywhere! everywhere!) will burn. Now acknowledge that none of that will last forever. If your workout is an hour long, this is just one tough hour in your life – that's nothing in the grand scheme of things. You've been through way harder shit than that. You can tough it out for sixty minutes.

If you want growth, change and development in your life, you can't stay comfortable. It's really as simple as that.

Tip: To get through those tough moments, remind yourself that this feeling of discomfort is temporary. You're not going to feel it forever; you just have to get through this moment.

Mantra: I've been through harder shit than this!

22. Trust your struggle

It's hard for a reason. There'd be no point if it was easy. Even the best athletes in the world struggle through their workouts. It's hard because there's beauty in the struggle. Diamonds are made under pressure, so you have to charge through the tough bits to get to the good. The struggle isn't there to highlight your weaknesses, it's there to guide you to your strength, tune you into your grit, develop your sense of 'no fucking way am I giving in now'.

The first time I attempted to run was at a parkrun, which are 5k runs that take place in parks all over the UK at 9 a.m. every Saturday. If you're not familiar with the world of distance running, 5k is the equivalent of three miles – bearing in mind that I had no reference point for how far one mile was, thinking I'd be able to run three of them on my first attempt was a little overambitious, to say the least.

I lined up at the start with a bunch of very keen-looking people in Lycra. Someone blew a whistle and we were off! I launched into a steady jog, arms swinging, feeling as if I looked just like those other runners out there. About twenty seconds in, my lungs were like 'WHAT ARE YOU DOING?!' as my legs slowly ground to a halt.

Everything in my body seemed vehemently opposed to whatever I was trying to do. But I'd barely even started. I had to finish the damn thing.

And that is when you find out exactly how long a mile is. Sweet. Baby. Jesus.

I made mini-deals with myself as I ran for a little, walked for a little, considered crawling for a while, fought back tears, genuinely wondered for a moment if one of my lungs had actually fallen out, was amazed that a stitch can last so long you consider having voluntary surgery for it. It was hard, so hard.

Then a pensioner overtook me and I figured this was some sort of cruel joke, that I was on a hidden-camera show that was making a mockery of my entire life. Then the girl in front of me threw up.

FOR THE LOVE OF GOD! WHY DOES ANYONE RUN?!

After what felt like hours, I was finally on the home straight. I stopped dragging my feet and put every last ounce of energy into getting to that finish line as fast as I could so this nightmare would be over.

It may have felt like hours, but it had actually only been thirty-five minutes. Running comes with some crazy kind of time warp, apparently.

I walked home that day a broken woman. But I couldn't let one run take me down like that.

The next week, I found myself back at the same start line in the park, ready to take on that 5k again. This time, I told myself I just wasn't going to stop. No matter how much it hurt, no matter how much my mind and body wanted to, I simply would not stop. The goal was to run the whole thing.

The whistle blew and I set off. I didn't panic as the seasoned runners breezed past me. I found a pace and locked into it. I chanted the words, 'I will not stop. I will not stop,' like a mantra in my head. My feet moved to the rhythm of that chant. Every time a thought floated into my head about the pain, or how it'd feel so much nicer to just walk right now, I chanted in my head a little louder, 'I WILL NOT STOP.'

People overtook me; I didn't care. I didn't feel fast or slow; I just revelled in my movement. Every step was one step closer. I had to do this. If I quit now, when would I ever see it through?

'I will not stop'.

And then, before I knew it, I came around the corner onto that last straight, finish line in sight. I picked my knees up and sprinted like my very life depended on it; my heart pounded, my lungs swelled and I crossed the line.

There was no medal, no ticker-tape parade, no marching band, but that one Saturday morning in a park in Leeds, I'd done something that just a week before had seemed impossible.

As I walked home, I had what Oprah would call an 'a-ha! moment'. It occurred to me that if I could push through those three miles when everything in me wanted to stop, what else could I do? What if I'd walked, in life, when I really could've kept running? I'd been selling myself short and cutting myself off for years.

That day, I resolved to approach everything in my life the way I approached that 5k run – I was just not going to stop. Whatever the situation – if it was hard, uncomfortable, seemingly impossible – I would just keep going until I got there.

And then, gradually, life started to change. As I went out on more runs, going a little further each time (just get to that next tree, that post box, that bus stop…), I became more focused, more driven, more confident. I was producing better work, I was pushing for what I wanted, drawing up plans for a life that I couldn't have imagined the year before. Every time I ran a little further or faster, it reassured me that I could do anything I put my mind to, if I just kept that level of focus.

You have to trust your struggle. Trust that it's more than this moment of breathlessness, these shaking muscles, the dread of having to do one more rep. Embrace it, own it – the struggle is where your story lies.

Tip: Refer back to your workout log. Read through all the tough workouts you've done and look at how you're still here, still living, breathing and bossing these sweat sessions. If you did it then, you can do it again.

Mantra: Greatness awaits on the other side of hardship.

23. Master the pep talk

If only you could carry Oprah or that really frikkin' peppy person from your office around in your pocket to give you motivational gems every day. As they're not always available, you're gonna have to learn how to master your own pep talk.

While personal pep talks might seem like you're just tooting your own horn, there's actually more to it than that. 'People who use pep talks, affirmations and mantras tend to be happier, healthier and perform better, in life and in sport, than those who hold negative views of themselves,' says Sarah Waite, psychologist and life coach.

Perfecting your pep talk may take a little practice. Here are Sarah's top five key ingredients to making yourself a good one.

1. Tune in to the truth
We hold all kinds of inaccurate, exaggerated 'truths' about ourselves and the world. Search for the real truth, and a more compassionate/loving angle:

a) Talk to someone who knows and loves you. And accept a kinder perspective.

b) Journal. Then pause. And tune in to your wiser, more loving self.

What's the real truth here? What's a more accurate/ compassionate/loving angle? What positive evidence do you have to back this up? See? Yes, you *are* amazing!

2. Make it personal
Start with 'I' or 'My'.

'I've got this!'
'My legs are a machine!'
'I'm an amazing cyclist!'

3. Be positive

Focus on what you will be and will do – no 'can't', 'won't' or 'don't'!

'I have great stamina!'
'I'm full of energy!'
'I run like the wind!'

4. Be present

Focus on the moment right now, not the future or result. More 'I am', 'I have' vs. 'I want', 'I will', 'I need', 'I can'.

'I'm unstoppable!'
'I'm powering up this hill!'
'I'm a natural-born runner!'

5. Keep your pep talk short and simple

The shorter the better, so they're easier to remember, repeat in your head, even write on your arm/leg/waistband to look at during a race or workout.

Get that Sharpie on standby!

'I'm strong!'
'I'm fast!'
'I feel good!'

But let's be real here: if your confidence and self-esteem have taken a battering and you're finding it tough to believe anything positive about yourself, the idea of a pep talk can be overwhelming or seem pretty pointless. How can we take some steps towards achieving some semblance of self-belief?

Sarah advises a few things:

Do the impossible

Pick a challenge, train, and go for it – the bigger and scarier the better!

When you face your fears and smash that seemingly impossible goal, suddenly everything is possible. You're unstoppable.

Crowdsource your self-belief

When you think of a rose, what do you see? Beauty, romance, love, bright colours, silky petals… you don't notice the thorns, discolourations and dog-eared leaves.

Your loved ones and friends see a rose-tinted version of you too.

Ask three friends: 'What are my skills, strengths and gifts?' Ideally, ask them to write it down for you to keep and treasure, and dig it out on days you need a boost.

Journal

Each morning, write three or more 'I am' statements based on positive things you know about yourself, nice things people say about you, or characteristics and qualities inspired by recent events. (You might struggle to start with, but persist.) For example: I am strong. I am persistent. I am healthy. I am creative. I am smart. I am resourceful.

Each night, write three or more great things you did today, and what that means about you. For example: I did thirty minutes at the gym (= I'm sporty, I'm strong, I'm energetic).

Try to be creative, using different descriptive words and examples.

It's a wonderful way to get to know yourself better and realise how amazing you are!

So, go and get some practice in. Stand in front of a mirror; tell yourself you're a badass. Now list the reasons why. Those reasons can be a celebration of whatever makes you feel better in that moment, be it getting up without the aid of an alarm, doing a morning meditation or cycling a hundred miles over the course of last week. Celebrate it regardless. Tell yourself why you're not going to give up today and what it means to you. Remind yourself of your ultimate goal and tell yourself, no matter how many times you need to, that you'll get there.

Now go get 'em, tiger.

Tip: Keep some motivational gems on deck – whenever you see or hear a quote or phrase that inspires you to do better, make a note of it. Jot it down in your phone or workout log so you can refer to it whenever you need a boost.

Mantra: I'm on a quest to be the best me I can possibly be.

24. It's OK to change your mind

Sometimes you find your 'thing' in fitness and throw everything you have into it. You find a workout you really love and it just becomes *life*. You talk about it all the time, arrange your life around it, get friends to do it with you, organise social events that incorporate it. You just love it with everything in you and then, one day, inexplicably, you just don't any more.

Let's take running, for example. I had a steady five-year love affair with running. Well, it wasn't all love, if I'm being totally honest. It started with a pretty intense hatred, downgraded to mild annoyance and after an epiphany or two, got elevated to euphoria and general runner-love smugness. I ran most mornings at 5 a.m., did half-marathon after half-marathon (and threw a couple of full marathons in there to keep things spicy). I was the go-to girl for all things running related. But then I went through a period of pretty big changes in my life and the love for running just… dwindled.

I beat myself up about it, tried in vain to get back out there, until I woke up one day and realised: I'm just over it.

I simply did not want to run any more. I didn't feel bad about it. I didn't feel conflicted. I didn't think it was a phase. I just had zero interest in it.

Running came into my life at a time I didn't realise I needed it. I was terrible at it. I couldn't understand why anyone would do it. Then, slowly but surely, I could run a little further each time, I got a little faster, I felt more confident, more self-assured, and my body was suddenly this powerhouse that made me feel like Wonder Woman every time I pounded the pavement.

I became part of a huge running community. Everyone I knew ran. We'd travel to other countries to run races together.

We were all bonded by this excellent and healthy pastime. Despite being part of this massive running community, I always preferred to run alone. Funnily enough, not many people fancied joining me on my 5 a.m. jaunts.

I did the London Marathon in 2015 and the training bored me almost to literal tears at times. Running can be pretty interesting up to about fourteen miles. After that, you get really envious of people waiting at bus stops.

I tried every kind of visualisation technique, I listened to podcasts, I ran in silence, I made playlists full of songs guaranteed to keep me going – I could not, for the life of me, find a way to stay interested.

And I never reached that higher plane of consciousness a lot of runners talk about either, where you're just watching the miles fly by and you're so focused on the moment. Nope. I was focused on a lot of other shit, mainly shit I'd rather be doing than trying to clock twenty miles on a cold Sunday morning.

I had a great time on race day. I danced my way around most of the route, but there was also a solid seven-to-eight-mile stretch of it where I was so bored, it took everything in me to not walk off the course and get on the nearest Tube.

Two days after the race, I was back on my spin bike, teaching. And that's where I felt I belonged.

Through the whole training process, that's where I experienced that sense of euphoria, a feeling of community. It's hard to wipe the smile off my face when I'm teaching spin.

A few weeks went by, then months. I'd had a few feeble attempts at little neighbourhood runs, but my heart wasn't in it.

The year after the marathon, exercise-wise, all I did was spin. I didn't miss running at all. I craved doing strength and flexibility work, but never really found myself longing for a run. And why would I? It's not like I wasn't getting enough cardio.

The way I see it, running, for me, was like any other relationship. Sometimes you find 'the one'; sometimes you drift apart and just have to move on.

Running represented a period of time in my life where I went through a lot, learned a lot, grew a lot and the miles I ran were an essential part of who I was.

They taught me so much about strength, resilience and confidence, about determination, self-worth and grit. I wouldn't trade those miles for anything.

But they are not who I am now. The thing with running is, you see gains fairly quickly. It's super-exciting to see that progression. When you go from just trying to make it from one lamp post to the next, to running a mile non-stop, to your first 5k – each of those moments is filled with excitement and pride. You can run further and faster every time. You sign up to races, you get all the medals, you train, you run with friends, you run when you're feeling low, you run to round off a great day. Your social media feeds are full of your love for running. People refer to you as 'that chick who runs'.

But what happens when the mojo goes? Who will you be if you're not 'the runner chick'?

Hear me and hear me now, amigo: you can change your mind any time you damn well please. Why do something that makes you miserable? Keeping exercise fun, exciting and varied is massively important. Don't ever feel tied to one particular activity, just because that's what people associate you with or expect you to do. If that particular workout is not bringing you joy, why keep pushing through it? That's a cycle that can lead to you hating exercise and we've just put in all this work getting you to love it!

Whatever it is that you're tired of, park it. Move on and try a different workout for a while, something that will spark some passion in you again.

You are allowed to change your interests, focus and goals any time you wish. Switch it up – keep 'em guessing.

Tip: Don't think of it as giving something up. It's creating room for opportunity, growth and learning.

Mantra: I have to be happy before I can make others happy. Changing my mind doesn't make me a quitter.

25. Your body is AMAZING

For too long, the narrative around fitness has been all about aesthetics. It's hard to break with the idea that you should be chasing a six-pack. But your body is so much more than that. If you study anatomy and physiology, even just a little bit, the inner workings of these shells we walk around in will blow your mind.

Wiggle your toes – seriously, do it right now. Do you understand the number of neurons that need to fire up in your brain and the millions of things that need to happen to get that message from your noggin all the way down to your feet?! We're walking miracles, goddamnit!

During your next workout, visualise what's happening inside your body. Think about your heart and lungs, think about the blood pumping through your veins, around your body, about your muscles contracting and relaxing. I always find focusing on the inner workings of my body helps me be present and gives me a whole new appreciation for movement.

Need a good example of this? Well, picture the scene: I'm on the Tube, making my way to ride a spin class to catch some Friday-night vibes. We pull into Tottenham Court Road station and an announcement is made that Holborn station (the next one, where I'll get off) is closed. Fine, I'll have to walk. But I'll be cutting it real fine, time-wise.

I jump off the train, weave through the crowds, run up the escalators, dodge more people, get through the ticket barriers, run up a flight of stairs and I'm out of the station. Time check: 4:51 p.m. Class starts at 5 p.m. and I need time to throw my stuff in a locker, change into spin shoes and set my bike up right.

So I take off running. I'm bobbing and weaving through

the heavy Oxford Street pedestrian traffic, I hurdle over a lazily pulled wheelie suitcase. At one point, there's a guy running towards me, in his work clothes, obviously in the same cutting-it-fine predicament as me: I jump into the bus lane and continue running so he can get past me without breaking stride. We smile at each other as this happens. 'Thanks!' he says. 'No problem!' I shout as I keep barrelling it down the road.

I come to a pedestrian crossing. Traffic is heavy and slow-moving. I don't have time for no green man, man! So I weave in and out of the cars, tiptoeing, light on my feet, navigating round double-decker buses and delivery vans. I make it to the other side unscathed.

Now I'm on the home straight. Heart pounding, heels kicking my bum, I'm busting out such a sprint. I'm Serena Williams in a Grand Slam final. I'm Paula Radcliffe in the last mile. I'm Nicola Adams before she knocks someone out. I cannot be stopped.

The spin studio is in sight. I charge through the doors and down the stairs; sweat dripping down my back, I'm panting so hard I can barely get my words out. I look at the staff behind the desk. 'Has it started?' I ask.

'Nah, five minutes 'til kickoff.'

And I think to myself how frikkin' lucky I am that my body lets me do that. I felt like She-Ra! Catwoman! I didn't care what I looked like while cracking out that crazy sprint, I was just amazed my body was doing it.

Whenever I doubt myself, my body's ability or what I can do, I just sit for a moment and wiggle my toes and just like that, I'm in awe!

Tip: Write down what it is about your body that you're grateful for. Think about it in very basic, physical terms. For example: 'I'm grateful that my core is getting stronger, so I can hold a plank longer.'

Mantra: Wiggle your toes!

26. There are people who expect you to quit

Whatever goal you've set yourself, there will be at least one person in your life who not only expects you to fail, but is secretly hoping it will happen. Every time you're out on a run, in a class or hitting up the gym, they're thinking, 'Yeah, yeah, but they'll quit eventually.' It's baffling that some people think that others pursuing a passion somehow threatens their personal growth, but alas, it can happen. Oftentimes that just stems from fear – someone else pushing forward in their life can serve as a reminder that perhaps you're not doing all you could with yours, so rather than it being an inspiration, it can fuel bitterness. Sure, that outlook says much more about the bitter person than it does you, but it doesn't mean you can't use it as fuel.

When you're in a particularly tough part of your workout, dedicate it to that person who doubts you. Think of them as you actively push yourself harder, further, better. Hope that they can someday find that strength for themselves. Wish them well with every bicep curl, sprint or burpee. You're doing something positive and by spreading those vibes, you can only hope that somehow it filters out into the atmosphere and rains down on that doubter… (or they choke on it, 'cause you know, fuck 'em! All depends on your perspective really.)

Tip: Turn their negativity into a positive for you. People will often be critical when they see others trying to improve themselves, usually because they don't have the courage or dedication to do it themselves. Set a good example of how your lifestyle change is having a positive impact on you.

Mantra: Haters gonna hate.

27. Big yourself up

You're allowed to be proud of yourself. Get acquainted with the art of the not-so-humble brag. You can acknowledge your achievements. Moreover, you can be vocal about them. If you've worked really damn hard to squat a certain weight and you finally achieve it, you should announce your greatness with the confidence of Kanye West at an awards show.

Don't just let the milestones fly by without acknowledging them. If you worked for it, you earned it, and you can take a moment to appreciate the graft you put in. Sometimes it feels like no one else notices, but that doesn't mean you should just sweep it under the carpet.

Whether it's a boastful Facebook update, or just getting a high five from someone in the class, heap a little praise on yourself for a job well done.

Tip: Be sure to write the feeling down in your workout logbook and call your fitness buddy – they'll be your cheerleading champion, for sure.

Mantra: Today I will not sweep aside my greatness!

28. See it, be it, achieve it

At the start of every workout, especially the tough ones where you know you're about to get your ass handed to you on a silver platter, take a moment, close your eyes and visualise how you want this to go.

Clearly picture how you want to feel at the end of it. Think about the sweat trickling down your back, the breathlessness, the race against the clock. Then think about the inside of your body and how hard it's working. Imagine the endorphins firing up in your brain and shooting around your body as you push it harder. See yourself smashing through the toughest parts of the workout, getting stronger, more determined, more focused with each passing second. Imagine yourself at the end of the class, sweaty, glorious and victorious.

Think about how you'll feel when it's all over: the confidence, the sense of achievement, the productivity and drive you'll have. Know that if you conquer this workout, you can conquer anything.

Then open your eyes and go kick some ass.

Tip: Give yourself a keyword or mantra you can repeat internally that'll help you push through the tough moments of the class. Mine's usually 'BADASS'!

Mantra: I am powerful beyond measure.

29. Change the way you speak about your body

My goodness, we can really be mean to ourselves, can't we? Nitpicking at a physical thing you don't like about yourself is a slippery slope. It starts with you lamenting your love handles and by the time you're done, you've convinced yourself you're an absolutely hideous, useless, friendless boil on the ass of society. Whoa! Whoa! Whoa! Easy, tiger! Let's take it down several notches.

For body-confidence coach Michelle Elman, being positive about her body came from a real sense of gratitude. 'I have had fifteen surgeries as a result of a brain tumour, a punctured intestine, an obstructed bowel, a cyst in my brain and a condition called hydrocephalus. I became really conscious of my body and more specifically, my scars,' she says. 'Body confidence was a long journey for me. It started back when I was fifteen and I decided to stop vocalising my negative opinions about my body aloud.

'Back then, I believed it was to avoid drawing more attention to my flaws, but now I realise that it actually shifted my focus away from the flaws themselves. I started just accepting that I should be grateful that I had a body, and that most people with my extent of medical interventions don't have the privilege of saying that. That's ultimately where my body positivity came from – a core fundamental respect for a body that keeps me alive and breathing every day.'

But if you're used to beating up on yourself all the time, the notion that you should just love every inch of your physique can be a tough one to grasp. 'If you don't genuinely believe what you're saying, then it's just fake positivity and that doesn't help anyone,' says Michelle. 'What helps is to be authentic to yourself and no matter how much you hate your body, everyone can find one thing they are grateful for.'

Exercise can be such a powerful force in changing the way you think and speak about your body. Central to that is disentangling nutrition and weight loss from the simple act of movement. 'The belief that a workout means we "deserve" food is really dangerous,' says Michelle. 'Once all the diet-culture messages surrounding exercise are removed, there is so much to love about movement. Fat women in particular are always taught to dissociate from their body, that their body is wrong and "the enemy". Movement can be a great way to teach someone how to be in their body and all about the power that lies within it.'

So, stop talking about all the things you'd like to physically change about your body and focus instead on what it can do. Talk about how muscly your thighs are, how long you can hold a plank, how great your stamina is, how strong you are. Let the ability of your body trump its aesthetics. All the negative things you say about your own body you'd never say to someone else about theirs, so why is it OK to be mean to yourself? Focus on the positives, your strengths, what makes you a total badass. Be a better friend to yourself – uplift and encourage.

Tip: Say five things that you love about your body out loud, right now. GO!

Mantra: I love my body!

30. Strong body, strong mind – stronger you all round

You already know that exercise isn't purely for your body. Hopefully, by this point in the book, you won't be so hung up on losing weight or chasing some kind of body ideal, because *yaaaawwwwnnnn*. Fitness is so much more exciting than that! That spring in your step, that boost in your productivity, that confidence you feel – these things aren't coincidences, you know!

You've been reaping the benefits of all those endorphins shooting around your body. Consistent training builds confidence, discipline, self-worth. Each time you push through a tough workout, you learn something about yourself, discover another barrier you were able to knock down, dispel another myth you'd come to believe. And every time you do that, you become stronger not just in your body, but in your mind and your overall sense of being.

Training today builds a stronger you for tomorrow in your mind, body and soul. Little by little, step by step.

Tip: Take a moment to reflect on changes you've seen in yourself outside of fitness since you committed to your workout regime. Are you more focused at work? Better able to keep commitments? Feeling more confident? Sleeping better? It's good to acknowledge the impact the sweat life is having on you outside of Lycra too.

Mantra: When I train my body, I train my mind.

If You're Flagging...

31. Just move more

Sometimes in fitness land it can seem that if you're not training for a marathon or World's Strongest Man competition you're just not doing enough. But not every day has to be a mammoth gym session.

Let's face it, we all have days where we just can't be arsed. We also have to be realistic – if you didn't sleep well, or did a really intense workout yesterday, your body isn't going to allow you to push those limits. But just because you feel like opting out of whatever workout you had planned today, it doesn't mean the day has to be a total exercise loss.

All forms of movement count.

So, while you may be too tired for your 10k training run, you could probably manage walking the dog for an hour, right? You might not feel like doing your weights session, but you could get off the bus a few stops early and walk the rest of the way home. And since you always eat lunch at your desk, why don't you mix it up today – get off your arse, get out in the fresh air and actually have a lunch break?

Tip: Take the stairs, take the long way, offer to help carry those heavy boxes – there are opportunities for you to build movement into your day all the time. Just because they don't take place in a gym doesn't mean they don't count. Just move more. Simples.

Mantra: All movement counts towards a healthier me.

32. Take it up a notch

Have you been cruising through your current workout plan? Able to complete it relatively easily, work up a bit of a sweat, feel accomplished but never really exhausted when you finish? No wonder you're feeling a bit bored! It's time to take it up a notch.

In your workout today, push everything a little further. Aim for a few more reps, a bit more distance, tiptoe out of the realm of the known and see what happens. Stop playing it safe. If you're cruising through your workout, you *know* you can do it. Now take a chance on yourself and see how far you can push it. Now you have an opportunity for real personal growth. There are some lessons awaiting you, somewhere in a pool of sweat, that you've been too comfortable to chase after. So let's ramp it up and see what happens! However small the progression, it's still progress. If you don't try, you'll never know.

Make a plan before you start. What's your new goal? What do you want to achieve in that session? How do you want to feel after it?

Tip: Invest in some sessions with a personal trainer – see how they create a plan for you to advance your abilities. It's important that you increase the level in whatever you're doing gradually. For example, if you have built up to running five miles, don't decide one day that you'll run ten! Ease into it: aim for six miles, do that a couple of times, then add another mile, and so on.

Mantra: I can, I will, I do.

33. Ditch your fitness tracker for the day

Wearable fitness trackers are très chic right now. You can track every waking second of your livelong day if you feel like it. Your wristband breaks down your heart rate, calories burned, steps walked and probably your blood type and the number of times you swore at your fitness instructor under your breath. It then collates all that info into fancy pie charts on an app on your phone.

Trackers are a great way to keep yourself motivated and try to push a little further. But sometimes it's good to just leave it at home for a day. Simply enjoy your love of movement without feeling the need to break down all your stats and compare, contrast, tweet, blog or Instagram them.

Just go for a run without thinking about how many miles you'll clock or where you'll end up. You won't throw your whole life out of sync if you don't know how many calories you burned today. In fact, I'm willing to bet good money that you probably don't even know what one calorie is. I sure as hell don't and look at me – living my life carefree! Also, it's worth noting here that a 2017 Stanford University study found that fitness trackers can be wildly inaccurate with the measurement of some of these variables. For example, a reading of how much energy is expended in a workout can be off by as much as 30 per cent on some devices – so while they can be a great motivational tool, take the stats with a hefty grain of salt.

Tip: Set different goals for a tracker-free workout: How many times did you smile during class? How many times did you swear? How many lamp posts did you run past? You can still make your session productive and interesting without having to measure serious stats.

Mantra: I am more than my stats!

34. Work out in the morning

You can work out at any time of day and it's best to go with what fits most easily into your life, but there are few things as powerful as an early-morning workout. A quality sweat session at the crack o' dawn sets the tone for your day. It wakes you up, clears your mind, gets you focused and powers up your energy.

Perhaps you're more of an evening workout person, but that way you have your whole day to talk yourself out of it, if you so wish. Doing it in the morning means it's done, over with and you can just crack on with your day knowing you were a total champion before it even got to 7.30 a.m. Imagine how much ass you'll have kicked by lunchtime!

Having a good morning sweat session has been proven to improve your mental focus and abilities for the rest of the day. Not only that, waking up and working out is a disciplined thing to do. You're prioritising your wellbeing right out of the gate, at the start of your day – and that lays the groundwork for you being the best you can be for the rest of your waking hours.

Tip: Give yourself the best shot at waking up to work out by powering down all your electronics about an hour before you go to bed. Read a book, write in your journal, do some colouring – anything to help your brain decompress from your day. Set your alarm and when it goes off in the morning, get up immediately. Do NOT hit snooze! Just get up, put your kit on and get out. Make yourself a playlist of songs you know are guaranteed to make you feel good and get you moving.

Mantra: Rise early, catch worms, kick ass.

35. Organise an old-school sports day with friends

Not every workout has to be a super-serious sweat-fest where you're pretending you're in an ad for a global sportswear brand (though it is pretty cool to do that). Some days you need to just forget the stats, break away from your regular workout, shake things up a bit, but mainly, make it fun.

Grab some friends and go and play rounders in the park, have an egg-and-spoon race, play tag, do a hundred-yard dash – then eat tons of food and act like lunatics after. It's not about the competition or upping your Fitbit stats, it's just purely for the love of movement, with the added bonus of it being a social gathering (and, of course, the bragging rights a win in rounders would bring).

Tip: The emphasis should be on FUN. Make it inclusive, accessible and varied. Having a silly kind of activities day serves as a good reminder of how much we just naturally moved as kids. You don't need fancy equipment or pricey gym memberships to get your heart rate up and have a good time.

Mantra: You're going DOWN! *said while pointing at opposing team* (finger guns and bicep flexing optional)

36. Do you, boo boo

Let's be clear, when it comes to your workout – how, when, where and with whom you choose to do it – you can be as selfish as you damn please. The opinions of others as regards your body, how it looks and how you use it are completely defunct. Don't work out for anyone else but you.

That guy at the gym who's always trying to correct your form when you're squatting? Yeah, fuck that guy. Unless he's a certified, qualified personal trainer, he can back right up outta your space and let you do your thing. Your 'thing' is whatever the hell you want it to be. If your favourite way to break a sweat is to do the running man to Vanilla Ice's 'Ice Ice Baby', turn the stereo up and get to it.

It's worth reminding yourself sometimes that while the fitness industry comes under the 'wellness' banner, there are segments of it that are rooted in us essentially not really loving ourselves. Huge amounts of money are spent nitpicking at us, telling us we shouldn't be happy with our bodies, or this workout is wrong and that one can do so much more for you.

Then here you come, all high on life, flinging your endorphins around, having a great time, feeling more than satisfied with your exercise regime – you are throwing a spanner in the works, amigo! Brands make way more money out of you when you're riddled with doubt and your self-esteem is at rock bottom.

If you like the way you do things, rock on. If and when you feel you need to seek help, guidance or assistance, go with that feeling and find someone you admire and trust to get you to the next level. As long as you're working out safely and not at risk of causing yourself injury, be at one with the bliss of doing things your own way.

Do not let the opinions of others deter you on your path to greatness.

Tip: Remind yourself that you make the rules for your body.

Mantra: Those who mind don't matter and those who matter don't mind.

37. Buy some new kit

Sure, it may be shallow, but it's a pretty basic fact that if you look good, you feel good, and somehow that makes you do better. Buying some new Lycra loveliness can give you exactly the motivational boost you need to get you out of an exercise rut.

A killer pair of leggings, new trainers, a flashy hoodie – whatever it is that floats your boat and makes you feel like a don when you put it on, treat yo'self and splurge on it. You'll feel so great, you'll make a point of scheduling a workout as soon as you can just to show off your new garms.

Tip: Do not, however, wear new kit for the first time when you have a race or some other challenge you've signed up to. You don't want to find out that it chafes or doesn't do its job right on a day that matters.

Mantra: Look good, feel good, do better.

38. Choose one exercise; become a Jedi Master in it

If your current workout regime has become a bit stagnant, you're not feeling it or you're just plain bored, it may be time to switch it up. Sometimes it really helps to pick one exercise and devote some time to becoming Jedi Master-level good at it. Be it pull-ups, squats, a certain yoga pose you've never quite managed to get – strip it right back to basics. Study it like a true student; learn all about correct form, then practise, practise, practise.

Having this laser focus on one particular move will not only build your skill set in that area, it'll do wonders for your general body awareness. Sometimes it's just good to slow down and go back to the beginning of something. We're all in such a hurry to just be great at everything, we often forget it takes time, patience and dedication. Be the Mr Miyagi to your inner Daniel-san.

Tip: If you have a friend, gym buddy or trainer you know who is great at whatever it is you want to get better at, get them involved, ask for their tips and see if they can give you some mini-goals to work towards in your progression.

Mantra: Slow and steady wins the race.

39. Drink more water

You're probably dehydrated right now. Did you know that your body can lose up to three litres of water through sweat, saliva and other bodily functions every day? And that's without you even busting into your serious sweaty workout mode.

We rarely consider how lucky we are in the Western world to have easy access to drinking water. And because we have such easy access to it, we don't give H_2O anywhere near the credit it deserves for being a magical unicorn of badassery every day.

Drinking water helps you feel more alert, improves your mood, treats headaches and migraines, flushes out toxins, helps digestive issues, regulates your body temperature, promotes healthy skin – the list of benefits is almost endless.

All too often the myriad of things we should be doing to keep ourselves fit and healthy can seem really overwhelming, but simply drinking more water is a pretty basic act of self-care.

So many of our general aches, pains and snuffles can be eased by drinking more water.

Tip: Keep a two-litre water bottle on your desk. With a black marker, draw a line about a quarter of the way down, another halfway down and another three-quarters of the way down. Set yourself time targets to hit each line: for example, top line – 10 a.m., middle line – 11 a.m., third line – 12 p.m., so you should've finished the bottle by 1 p.m. If you're working out that day, be sure to drink more.

Mantra: Water is life!

40. Take it down a notch

Earlier, we talked about ramping your workouts up, but if you've been hammering these workouts and are feeling frustrated over it, like you've plateaued, or you've found yourself randomly crying in the supermarket for no reason at all, you may need to step back a bit. Those feelings are always a sure sign that something needs to change. Rather than beat yourself up about it and try to push harder, what you really might need is to just take it easy for a couple of days.

Scale back the workouts a little. If you've been going to town on the hard stuff like weights, maybe you need to lift lighter, slow down a bit and really zone in on your form, rather than constantly trying to go heavier.

If you're slaying HIIT sessions consistently and are feeling tired, take your foot off the gas and do a stretch and flexibility class or some nice yoga practice. You don't need to be going a hundred miles an hour every day. It's nice to slow down, use your body in a different way – it's like hitting reset, so you can come back stronger.

Tip: If you're feeling overtired and run-down, that's a sign that you might have been pushing yourself too hard. Take a rest day – the world won't stop if you do. When you're tired, you're more likely to injure yourself.

Mantra: Breathe, stretch, release.

For Your Spirit

41. Go and watch a marathon

Feeling deflated and lost your mojo? Go and watch a marathon. I'm of the belief that everyone should run a 26.2 at least once in their life, but if you can't do that, you should *definitely* go and watch one. Nowhere else will you witness this level of grit, determination and spunk.

You're a fit person, so you can understand what's involved in training for one of these gruelling races. Knowing that makes it even more of an honour to watch. Every single person running has climbed a proverbial mountain to even make it to the start line.

From the Kenyan elites to the guy with a fridge on his back, you will see every body type, every speed, every emotion. Each one of them fighting their own personal battle, finding their own reasons to carry on, step by step.

If that doesn't light a fire under your ass and inspire you to nail your next workout, nothing will.

Tip: Don't just watch – cheer! Make signs, bring sweets to hand out to runners who need a sugar hit, clap enthusiastically – they're doing something pretty incredible, so act accordingly!

Mantra: Encouraging others keeps me encouraged.

42. You won't love every workout

And that's totally OK. Some days you'll end your workout feeling like Rocky bounding around at the top of those steps, other days you'll just feel a bit 'meh'. Don't let one lacklustre workout kill your whole vibe. It's tempting to get *Dynasty*-level dramatic about it when you have a crappy workout. Try to avoid throwing yourself on couches while declaring, 'It's just no use! I'll never be able to do a burpee!'

It's just one bad workout. Tomorrow is a new day when you will have new energy and a fresh mindset. Don't let it make you doubt why you started this journey in the first place. Just chalk it up and move on. You don't need to have a major life epiphany every time you work out. You won't always finish the cool-down and suddenly be spouting Dalai Lama-esque gems of wisdom. Sometimes a workout is just a workout – no bells and whistles, no life-changing wonderment. It doesn't invalidate the work you put in. Loads of factors can contribute to a crappy workout: stress, tiredness, anxiety, loss of focus. You're human; it happens. Even Superman had to be Clark Kent sometimes.

Tip: Have a think about the factors that may have thrown your workout off a bit. Our immediate instinct is often to think, 'I'm crap!' But think about external factors and see if you can work on minimising the impact they might have on your workout days in future.

Mantra: One bad workout doesn't define me.

43. Kill two birds with one stone

So many things come under the banner of 'wellness' – mindfulness, meditation, exercise, healthy eating – the aim being to be at a 'state of complete physical, mental and social wellbeing', to use the technical definition. With everything else that life throws at us, managing to do just one of those things can seem insurmountable at times. I've always found that the right exercise session can bring elements of mindfulness and meditation in there, so you can kill two birds with one stone.

An early-morning run, for example, brings real moments of clarity, where you can focus on nothing but your footsteps or your heartbeat. You can take the time to be aware of your surroundings, acknowledge everything that's happening in your body – those are the types of cues you'll get in a meditation session and you can do all that while clocking some meaningful miles.

'There's an interesting perception that mindfulness can only be achieved by sitting in silence or while chanting, with crossed legs and your hand in a mudra [touching the index finger to the thumb],' says yoga teacher Michelle Holmes. 'While that can be true if the life you're living allows that on a regular basis, to practise mindfulness and get the benefits in our society and environment, stillness and focus needs to be achieved in other areas of life.'

Michelle believes everything can be done in a mindful way. 'To me, mindfulness is to be out of your mind, out of being embroiled in the negative and critical self-talk and internal chatter, and fully occupy the moment. In yoga we move and breathe on the mat while we get in and out of postures, and this prepares us to move and breathe in our every day in this same manner,' she says.

'Working out is no different. By focusing on the breath, how it moves in and out and how our movements correlate with this, whether we are swimming or running, we are being mindful – paying attention to the here and now, present with what is. Our bodies do so much for us daily, and exercising while being fully in the present can be us paying homage to our bodies in deep reverence and appreciation of all that they can do.'

But finding mental focus and clarity can be such a struggle during a workout. If you get too inside your head, before you know it, you can talk yourself right out of whatever exercise you were just about to do. What do you do when you're struggling?

Michelle says to just breathe. 'Our lives are so full of movement and activity and our minds are often moving at such a fast pace, thinking about something that has happened or what we need to do later, it's no wonder mental clarity is hard to find,' she says. 'Not judging ourselves when we do find ourselves caught up in the chatter is important, as that takes us further into the mind and out of our bodies in the moment. Focusing on breathing, taking considered breaths in and out deeply, helps to deepen our workout and allows us to connect with the physicality of what we are doing.'

The best part is that by practising that peace and mindfulness through movement and exercise, you'll soon find it fans out into other areas of your life and you're better able to cope with other situations life throws at you.

'A lot of our mental ill health in society at large comes from dwelling on the past or anxiety about the future, because everything is so fast-paced,' says Michelle. 'Mindfulness in our daily life allows us to do our daily activities with more ease and grace, more patience and attention to detail. Everything is done in a more effective way when we are focused and present. This can be challenging when we start, but like any practice, it can become habitual over time.'

What exercise can do for your mind is just as important as what it can do for your body.

Tip: Choose studios, times of day and workouts that will help you tap into your mindfulness. It can be hard to find your Zen in a packed class pumping European techno at eardrum-busting levels.

Mantra: Today I'll work out my mind while I work out my body.

44. Gratitude

Ever stop to think how frikkin' amazing your body is? You spend a lot of time putting it through the ringer with your crazy workouts. It's easy to get mad at your body for the things it won't do (yet), but it's worth taking time out to have a moment of gratitude for all it is doing every day. Appreciate how hard your heart, lungs and muscles work to power you through a workout – hell, appreciate how hard they work just to get you standing upright every day. We always take it for granted, until we're injured, when all of a sudden we're made hyperaware of what a finely tuned machine the human body really is.

Before I got into exercise, I never really thought about my body. I wasn't doing anything exceptional with it. Lying on a couch for extended periods of time doesn't require any particular talent. It was my mind that cried out for movement before my body did. I just got so bored with feeling 'blah' and lethargic. Somehow, my mind convinced me that movement would shake things up in my brain.

Your brain is one smart cookie. You should listen to it.

As I mentioned before, my first exercise session was at a boxing gym in Leeds. I had no business being there. I got winded walking up the one flight of stairs to the gym. I didn't own hand-wraps or gloves and had no idea what to expect. But the second that bell rang and everyone around me leapt into action, churning out endless sit-ups, press-ups and burpees, I just joined in. I was breathless within seconds, but it sparked an excitement in me. I was so giddy to just be doing something, no matter how hard I was finding it, that I was determined to persist.

An hour and a half later, I'd learned how to throw a punch and I threw many of them into pads and heavy bags. The trainer even identified I had the beginnings of a pretty mean right hook. My chest swelled with pride.

By the end of the session, I could barely stand. My arms felt like two limp bits of spaghetti, my legs wouldn't stop shaking and, if I sneezed, I'd wince at the pain that shot through my abs. But the one thing I felt? Grateful. I'd made it through. Not only that, I'd made it through after years of actively avoiding doing anything that'd make me break a sweat. I felt grateful that my body had let me do any of it at all. I was proud of myself for having the guts to walk into the gym, somewhat stunned that I'd stayed for the entire session, but mainly just thankful.

For the first time in a long time, I didn't feel 'blah'. I felt alive again, excited, curious about what else my body would allow me to do. I had a newfound respect for my heart, lungs and muscles. I'd spent so long convincing myself that exercise just wasn't for me, all without even bothering to actually try, that I was completely bowled over at what my body had allowed me to do.

The human body is amazing. Treat it accordingly and heap some praise upon it today.

Tip: Take a few moments to just sit and think about what your body can do now compared to when you first started to get fit. Even if it's just a small improvement, it's something to be grateful for. Maybe treat your body to a massage as a thank-you.

Mantra: My body is awesome!

45. Rest, recover, revive

Don't be one of those nutters who throws a tantrum if they can't work out one day. You may well love it, you may be totally in your zone and hitting target after target with your training, but you still need to rest and let your body recover. This isn't optional. You can try to be the hero and push through day after day, but eventually your body will let you know one way or another that it needs you to give it a damn break every now and then.

Or, you can push yourself to the point of exhaustion or injury and be involuntarily sidelined for way longer than you needed to be, if only you'd just taken that damn rest day.

Your choice!

Osteopath Mark Hokan says recovery should be taken as seriously as your training, as it has the potential to really improve your performance.

'The aim of recovery is to allow your body to replenish what it needs physiologically and psychologically between workouts,' he says. On a physical level, Mark points out that happens in four main ways:

1. The normalisation of physiological functions (so, your blood pressure and cardiac cycles levelling back out).
2. Return to homeostasis (a fancy term for the regulation of the conditions within your body, such as temperature, water content, carbon dioxide levels and all that jazz).
3. Restoration of your energy stores (your blood glucose and muscle glycogen store up all the energy you need to fuel a workout, so after a good sweat session, it just stands to reason that you give them a little time to replenish).
4. Allowing time for muscles to repair.

If the body is never allowed time to achieve those things, you're never going to hit your training goals.

So how can you tell if you're not getting enough recovery? 'Initial signs to look out for are fatigue, apathy towards your workouts, persistent muscle soreness or joint pain, lack of gains and lowered immunity,' says Mark.

The type of recovery that's best for you all depends on the type of training, length of time between sessions and what is available to you at the time. Mark has five go-to faves that he recommends most often:

Massage: 'It's beneficial in the psychological benefits of recovery,' Mark says. 'And it increases blood flow, which helps to improve the clearance of metabolic waste [substances that build up in your muscles during a workout].'

Sleep: 'Create a good sleep routine; don't watch TV or use your computer in bed,' advises Mark. 'Avoid caffeine four to five hours before going to bed too.'

Active Recovery: 'This is low impact aerobic exercise. The idea is to increase blood flow which will help clear out lactic acid and metabolic waste that builds up in the muscles.'

Compression garments: 'The compression reduces space for swelling to build up,' says Mark. 'It'll promote muscle stability and therefore reduce muscle soreness.'

Nutrition: 'Replenishment of carbohydrates and protein is key post-exercise, along with fluids to help optimise muscle-damage repair.'

Tip: Use the recovery day as a reward. Plan to do something, so it's a treat you can look forward to.

Mantra: Recover now, be awesome later.

46. Get a sports massage

You've probably gotten so used to muscle soreness that you just consider it the norm at this point. But you should be able to walk up and down stairs without wincing 'cause your calves and hamstrings are so tight. When you get out of bed in the morning, you shouldn't be moving like a tin man.

Keep your muscles loose; show them some love. They work hard for you and you put them through a lot. The least you can do is treat them the way they deserve to be treated. Let a sports-massage therapist lay their magical hands on you, easing the pain out of your muscles so they can fight even harder for you the next day.

Disclaimer: I should point out that a proper sports massage isn't a pleasant experience at all. If you're expecting candles, low lighting and whale music, you're in for the shock of your life. A sports massage is painful – you'll wince, you may even swear a time or two, but you'll come out of there feeling like a whole new person.

Tip: Use your massage therapist's knowledge and expertise. Tell them to focus on a particular area that's been bothering you, ask them for any tips they might have on how to ease pain or good stretches to do for that area.

Mantra: This massage is a necessity, not a luxury!

47. Be present (PUT YOUR DAMN PHONE AWAY!)

In the world of #Instafit, you may feel it's a requirement to record every moment of your workout. Hell, I even advised you to do it back in Chapter 19 – every now and then, it's nice to document what you're doing and it can help you view your workout in a new way. But you know it's OK to leave your phone out of it too, right? In fact, you'll find you get a better workout when you do. If you're constantly thinking about Snapchatting and Instagramming your sit-ups, squats and downward dog, you're not focused on what you're doing. You can't be fully present in the moment, engaged in and embracing what your body is doing if you have this bit of technology blocking your view the whole time. Not to mention that a momentary lapse of concentration while you choose the best filter for that pic could lead to you getting injured.

Our constant connectivity and addiction to technology is a problem. If you can't put your phone away for an hour to get a good workout in, that's something you should be concerned about. Time away from your phone is essential. Grant yourself an hour or so free of notifications, emails, work-related stress and constantly being contactable. Once you do, you'll appreciate just how nice an hour with no distractions can be.

Tip: Use your workout as an opportunity to be mindful. The world will not end if you don't have your phone glued to your hand for sixty minutes. Put it in your locker and allow yourself to be free of calls, texts, emails and notifications for that time. Remember, your workout is your time to focus on YOU. Stop being a slave to your phone!

Mantra: I don't have to live by the 'pics or it didn't happen' philosophy.

48. This is YOU time

If you have no other time to yourself in the day, let your workout be that time. We sacrifice so much of our day to work, friends, chores, various other adult commitments that the moments we get to just hold court with ourselves, check in, nourish our soul, tune in with our bodies are few and far between.

Use your workout as a sacred time to convene with yourself. Be truly, utterly selfish in your want and desire to carve out that time and connect with your inner warrior. There's something wonderful about focusing on the simple pleasure of movement. It's primal. It strips you back to who you are; it can be both vulnerable and powerful. It loads you up with the purest elements of yourself that you'll need to manage the stresses of your life.

Showing up for yourself is not only important, it's essential. We have a myriad of people and things commanding our attention every day, which can take us further and further away from our own needs. Using your workout as time to focus purely on the betterment of you allows you to be your best for everyone else.

See? You sweat a bit and everybody wins!

Tip: Be unashamed of taking the time for yourself. Put your phone away and let any other commitments know they'll have to wait until you're finished with your sweat session. Remind yourself how much better you feel when you've taken that time for you.

Mantra: I'm not being selfish – I'm taking care of myself.

49. Make yourself a mood board

It takes a little while to form a habit and there will be days (probably many of them) mingled in there where you just don't want to do it. That's why it's a good idea to literally look at the bigger picture.

Sit down and make a mood board for yourself, not just about fitness but about what this journey means for you on a whole bunch of levels. If you're not familiar with mood boards, here's your chance to channel into your arts and crafts side. Get a piece of paper or card and whenever you come across images, phrases, words in magazines that inspire you or speak to you, tear them out and stick them on your board. What do you want your life to look like? What are the benefits of you being fit? How will your newfound confidence manifest itself? What will you be more driven to do that you haven't done before?

Mood boards of mine have included powerful women standing at podiums delivering speeches, beautiful cottages in Canada, images that represent calm and stillness, sometimes huge piles of cash (when I'm broke and want to manifest some money!).

Mood board it all out, so on those days when you doubt yourself, don't feel like getting up or would like to drop-kick your personal trainer directly in the chest, you can remind yourself that this whole thing is bigger than this singular moment of doubt.

Tip: There is no right or wrong way to create a mood board. Don't question what you should put on there. If it feels right to you and is an accurate representation of what you want for yourself – go for it!

Mantra: If I can see it, I can be it.

50. Have a list of inspirational YouTube clips to watch

There's something about watching the struggle of pro athletes do their thing that will light a fire under your ass to get out there and go give your best. On days when I need an extra boost, I line up clips of some of my favourite sporting moments on YouTube. They're usually set to some music that stirs your soul in such a way that you'll feel immense pride, be moved to tears or want to try out for the next Olympics.

When you're used to consistently training your body, you can understand the level these athletes need to be at to get on the world stage and exactly how much work it took them to get there. If they can do that, you can make it through whichever forty-five-minute class you've lined up today.

Some of my faves are: Kelly Holmes winning two gold medals in the 2004 Olympics, Mo Farah's 5000m win at London 2012, and the Dick Beardsley/Alberto Salazar showdown at the end of the 1982 Boston Marathon.

Tip: Sometimes you can get the motivational hit you need from something that's not even sport-related at all – there are tons of TED talks I've found that give me a boost when I need them. Get your inspiration in whatever form it comes.

Mantra: Watching greatness inspires me to be great.

Premium Pep Talks

51. This is about so much more than your body

If every other chapter of your workout journey has been about trying to get your body to look a certain way – your wish for slimmer thighs, a perkier butt, flatter stomach, more toned arms – let today be the day you write a new story.

Let today be the day you look at the cellulite on your legs and remind yourself that those legs have deadlifted serious weight, or clocked mucho miles. Your less-than-toned arms have gone round after round on a heavy bag, or powered you through that one last push-up despite shaking and fatigue.

You are getting stronger, better, bolder, braver with every bead of sweat, every breathless pant, every muscle twitch. That confidence you feel when you finish your workout is carrying over into every other area of your life. You're walking taller, you're smiling more, you're more focused. Your colleagues have noticed there's something different about you. It's your swagger. You move like you can scale mountains for breakfast, take on Tyson at lunch and downward dog your way through dinner.

You can hate on your body all you want, but it doesn't change the fact that you're a badass. Every time you and your not-so-perfect body get out there, you're inspiring someone who hasn't had the confidence to try yet – they were waiting for someone like you, so they could see that if you can do it, maybe they can give it a try.

So fuck trying to get a 'perfect' body. Fuck aiming for perfect, ever. Fuck stereotypes and self-doubt. Fuck the demonisation of curves and fat rolls. Fuck the constant message that you, as you are right now, just showing up, isn't good enough.

This journey is about so much more than your body. It's about showing up for yourself, finding your grit, staying the course, choosing to push through your self-doubt rather than succumb to it. It's about accepting and embracing yourself at your most vulnerable, it's about practice: trying, failing and trying again. It's about showing yourself that no matter how much you want to give up on you, you never, ever will. This is you understanding that you are worth all this effort.

Now, what was that you were saying about your cellulite?

Mantra: My capacity for greatness is infinite.

52. What do you gain by quitting?

So what do you stand to gain by quitting? Seriously. I'll wait.

You knew this wasn't going to be easy when you got into it. Everyone can do easy stuff – people do it all damn day. But you started this for a reason. On some level, you want to test your limits, push your boundaries, discover something about yourself that you haven't tapped into yet. So, if you quit, you won't ever find out.

All that potential stirring inside you – you just wanna leave it there? You don't wanna show yourself and the world exactly how much of a badass you can be? You don't want to take the lessons you learn on the gym floor and march that confidence straight into the boardroom with you?

Quitting's a cop-out. All the things you could gain from this workout, you're willing to throw away without trying? Everyone has a million and one reasons they can quit every day. You weren't built for that. The difference between being average or exceptional today is pretty easy – you just have to show up. Just try. You've faced harder decisions, you've done harder workouts, life has thrown worse things at you than this moment of self-doubt.

Quitting is so boring. It lacks adventure and excitement, and you don't want that kind of life. Think of yourself on your best day, when you smashed through your workouts with a vigour Serena Williams herself would struggle to keep up with. Think of yourself on your worst day, where you struggled to get out of bed and your self-doubt had you in a choke hold. Do either of those versions of you deserve to be given up on in this moment?

We *know* you can quit. Quitting's easy. But you're made of

stronger stuff. Take one more chance on yourself today and find out just how incredible you can be.

Mantra: I will NOT give up on myself today.

53. Nothing happens overnight

There is no quick fix. All those magazine covers you've seen touting 'Twenty-One Days to Rock-Hard Abs!' are bollocks. You won't be the Dalai Lama after a couple of meditation sessions, nor will you have mastered the art of Zen after a week of yoga. We're all in such a rush to be the best at everything. You may be the CEO in your office, but in your boxing class you're the newbie who can't quite make it through a round yet. That's totally OK. Everyone in there was once the newbie too.

Not nailing your goal today doesn't mean you never will. Someone else reaching their goal before you doesn't negate your efforts. We're living in a world full of convenience, where we can have whatever we want at the click of a button, but there's no shortcut to physical and mental change. You just have to put the work in; steady, consistent, dedicated work.

Slow down. Trust the process. You will get there. This is the good bit – the learning, the struggle, the overcoming, the figuring it out. This is where the lessons lie. This bit matters. Don't worry about being perfect or great or even good. Just focus on showing up and doing whatever your best looks like *today*. You will get there.

Patience, young grasshopper.

Mantra: Be the best me I can be today.

54. However hard your workout is, you've been through harder shit than this

I hear you. Your workout today is super-tough. Let me wipe the sweat from your brow while I remind you of a few things.

Have you ever bought a house? Ever had a career-changing promotion rest in the hands of someone who absolutely hates you? Suffered a death in the family? Gone through a break-up where your ex was that particular brand of petty whereby they'd rather chainsaw every last book in half than let you keep something?

Yeah, *those* things are hard. *Those* things are stressful. And yet, somehow, your badass self managed to get through them. Why? 'Cause you're tough, 'cause you glide through pressure like the finest of swans, that's why.

Life throws ridiculous situations at us all the time. You'll be in the midst of it, thinking, 'I don't know how I'm going to deal with this,' and all the while you're managing it, navigating it, figuring it out. You simply adjust.

In 2016, my beloved dog, Stringer Bell, was diagnosed with advanced lymphoma and given a couple of months to live. I was beyond devastated. I was crying so much during that time, I thought I might flood my flat. But despite feeling as though my heart was literally breaking, I got him to all his vet's appointments, I taught seven spin classes a week, I kept to all my commitments and I loved him harder than I ever had. I didn't think at the time how much energy it was taking for me to even be upright, I just carried on. Because that's what we do. What other choice do we have when the going gets tough? Life still continues. We don't get to hit pause while we try to figure things out.

My pup passed away three months after diagnosis and

I was back teaching spin the day after he was put down. I sobbed before, during and after my classes, but I did them. I needed to do them. They gave me a place to channel my pain. Now when I'm struggling in a workout, I think of him and that precious three months at the end of his life. I think how he fought on through his illness and all the things I did to keep him as happy and comfortable as I could. It was the hardest thing I've ever been through, but it taught me just how strong I can be.

There is no workout I will ever face that will be harder than making the decision to put Stringer Bell down. If my mind, heart and soul can get me through that, my body can sure as hell get through this workout.

You are stronger than you can ever imagine. Sometimes you don't realise exactly how strong that is until you come out the other side. Think back to the most challenging thing you've dealt with, where the stress, hurt or heartache was off the charts. Remember how you pulled through it and managed it like a boss.

And you're trying to tell me you can't do another press-up today? GET OUTTA HERE!

Mantra: I have endured and overcome, and I will again.

55. Do it to stick it to the patriarchy

Since the dawn of time, the patriarchy has dictated how we're supposed to look and act. Women weren't officially allowed to run marathons until the 1970s because some bros thought our uteruses would fall out. True story. From corsets in Victorian times to implants in the 1980s and injecting Botox in your face in the 2000s, the female form has been constantly policed. Working out and getting sweaty was deemed terribly unfeminine. God forbid we don't put our attractiveness at the top of our list of priorities every second of the goddamn day.

The pressure we have to look perfect all the time is unreal. Every time you've shied away from a workout because your cellulite shows through your leggings, you think you look too bloated, you don't like the way your arms look in that top, you're worried about your makeup sweating off, you're embarrassed about how much your face glows when you get sweaty – understand that you feel that way because as women, we've been conditioned for decades, nay centuries, to believe that for us to look anything other than perfect at all times just won't do.

How ridiculous is it that we're nervous to just show up as ourselves? All this faffing around worrying about our vanity – if it's stopping us from working out, it's literally putting our health at risk. How nuts is that?!

So, you see, you have to work out today to take your power back, to define for yourself what a beautiful, strong, sexy-as-hell body looks like on your own terms. Get sweaty, let your face glow, be competitive, grunt while you lift that weight if you have to – it's an act of defiance. Don't shrink; don't surrender your space.

Your body. Your rules.

Mantra: I am woman, hear me roar!

56. Look how far you've come!

In 2013, I was invited to ride L'Étape du Tour, a mountainous stage of the Tour de France that they open to the public. I had never ridden a road bike before. At the time, I was heavily into running and a cycling brand approached me to do the challenge to encourage more women into the sport and to see how a runner would adapt to cycling training. That year, there were around 13,000 people signed up to race – 700 of them were women.

I didn't blend in to the cycling community very well. I sucked. Considering the entire point of the event is that it's a mountainous course, I was absolutely terrible at going up hills. For six long, hard months I trained pretty much solo. I had no clue what I was doing.

Training for an endurance event is hard enough as it is but, man, this one was particularly lonely. I was completely out of my element. Somehow I had to prepare to cycle up mountains that frikkin' professionals find tough on *their* best day. It was incredibly hard to keep my head in the game and not get completely discouraged.

I landed in France the day before the race. A guy asked me if I was riding it and I said yes. He looked me up and down and said, 'But you are too big, *non*?' Like, straight up told me I was too fat to be riding a bike.

But this blazing hot day in July 2013, I cycled up some mountains. I cycled 'til my legs screamed and my lungs felt like they'd fall out. I got off at one point and *carried* my goddamn bike, 'cause FUCK IT.

It took me hours. I hallucinated. I cried. I cursed whoever's stupid idea it was to even invent bikes in the first place, but I bloody well finished it.

When I first started training for that event, I thought it'd take a miracle to get me through the course. You'd be hard pushed to find someone worse on a road bike than me the first six weeks of that training. But I kept at it and, little by little, I got better. As I approached the finish line on race day, I couldn't believe how far I'd come (and I'm not talking about the 130 km of the race).

Moments of doubt are inevitable. If you feel stuck in a rut and have lost your mojo a bit, it always pays to just reflect for a second on how much you've achieved thus far. Think back to the you of three months ago, six months ago, a year. What can you do now that you couldn't then? What has changed in your life as a result of you just being more active? Look at the bigger picture – are you more confident, more self-assured? Do you stand up for yourself?

Then look at your physicality – are you stronger, faster, more flexible? Where do you feel you've made the most gains?

It's unlikely that you've made no progress at all. Whether you've managed to climb some mountains on your bike, or you've mastered your pull-up form, celebrate your wins, no matter how small they may seem. Every little bit matters.

And just imagine where you'll be a year from now.

Mantra: I'm getting better every day.

57. Be Beyoncé at Madison Square Garden

Are you gonna do the shrinking violet thing, where you doubt yourself and your capabilities for your whole life? 'Cause surely you must get bored of that at some point.

What would happen if you stopped fearing who you could be and just allowed yourself to be the very best version of yourself? Are you scared you're gonna be *too* awesome? Will it be just too much for the rest of us to take? Well, bring it on! We'll deal with it!

How does it benefit you, or anyone around you, to be shrinking yourself? I mean, go ahead and keep telling yourself you're not capable if you want, but before you know it, your whole life will have passed you by and you won't have shit to show for it. If you hold back on this workout today, you're holding back on other things in your life. And we deserve to see you shine, damnit!

So, for the love of God, can you get out of your own way for a second? Can you stop throwing excuses around and telling yourself you're not good enough? Stop waiting for the perfect set of circumstances and live for this, right here, right now.

Don't just walk into your class today, strut in there like you're Beyoncé at Madison Square Garden. Stomp right to the front, flick your ponytail and let your presence make everyone know you are about to OWN. THIS. SHIT.

Channel the very spirit of Bey. Accept no second-rate shit from yourself today. Push harder, go further, be stronger, do better, demand more from yourself.

Mantra: It's my time to shine.

58. I AM somebody

I AM somebody.

However much I tell myself I'm done, I keep showing up for myself.

However much I want to give in, I'm still here.

When it comes to getting through my bad days, I have a 100 per cent success rate.

For anyone who's ever hurt me, tripped me up or put me down, fuck you. The joke's on you – you didn't break me. I'm getting stronger every damn day.

Even on the days when it feels like my self-doubt might cripple me, somewhere deep inside me something tells me to keep going.

Whatever challenge has been thrown at me, I have overcome.

Through every battle, every struggle and every time I've wanted to lay down my sword, my spirit got up and told me to fight.

I can't be held back.

I'm tired of cheating myself. I'm tired of leaving my potential up for grabs. I'm tired of not believing I'm worth it.

Today will be different. I will not settle for a second-rate version of myself. I won't live in muted tones. I won't deny myself the opportunity to find out exactly how great I can be.

So consider this me getting out of my own way. Through sweat and breathlessness and endorphin-fuelled euphoria, I'm going to honour the me *I know* I can be.

Because I am so very worth it.

Because I AM somebody.

Mantra: I'm destined for badassery and refuse to hold myself back.

59. It's allowed to be fun!

Lest we forget that you're actually allowed to enjoy your workouts and the feeling of being healthy. Forget 'earning your food' or trying to burn it off, counting calories or punishing your thunder thighs into submission.

Your sweat time isn't meant to be some sort of punishment. It is actually allowed to be fun. You are allowed to enjoy it.

Stop doing workouts you hate! What's the point? So you can convince yourself that exercise just isn't for you? Absolute nonsense!

Stop worrying that you don't look like a total pro while doing your workout. Who gives a shit? Whose business is it, other than yours, what your body looks like and what you're doing with it?

Find workouts you like, do more of them. It's been scientifically proven that the more you smile during a workout, the more effective it is (OK, I just made that up, but whatever). You can be silly, you can laugh at yourself, you can giggle when you can't nail that yoga pose that everyone else is getting. Better to laugh at yourself than work yourself up into a frustrated frenzy that makes you jack it in.

Enjoy it, be playful, let your inner child experience the wonder of learning new ways to use your body. There are plenty of other things to be serious about in life, a myriad of mediocre, adult-y bollocks that can be a total snooze-fest. Don't make your workout one of them. Smile your way through that bad boy!

Mantra: I am at my best when I allow myself to step into sweaty greatness.

60. This is about more than getting sweaty

This is about showing your high-school PE teacher they were wrong to doubt your rope-climbing abilities. It's about showing your boss you know all about commitment. It's about proving that you don't give up so easily, that you actually do want the best for yourself. It's about showing your ex that life is just peachy without them. It's about wanting to be healthy and active for as long as you live. It's about setting an example for everyone around you. It's about being a leader, a warrior, a badass bitch who don't take no shit. It's about rejecting your negative internal dialogue, because you're tired of hearing yourself whine. It's about learning to love your flushed, sweaty face. It's about accepting less than perfect. It's about continually showing up for yourself. It's about understanding that you can change the narrative of your life whenever you damn please and that exercise has been a primary driver in giving you the focus and dedication to do that. It's about loving how you look naked and marvelling at how wondrous your body is. It's about giving yourself the room, space and permission to grow. It's about letting yourself be vulnerable and being comfortable with where that takes you. It's about coping mechanisms and fighting through your down days. It's about empowerment, sticking it to the patriarchy, claiming the greatness of the body you inhabit.

Embrace it all. Choose to make it about the good.

Mantra: Greatness oozes from my very pores.

Acknowledgments

This book wouldn't have been possible without the guidance and patience of Richard Pike, Scott Pack and Ella Chappell.

Huge thanks to Camilla Henderson, Kim Ngo, Rachel Tran, Laura Lakam, Michelle Holmes, Sarah Waite, Mark Hokan and Michell Elman for sharing their infinite wisdom in these pages.

Thanks to Tom Street for the motivational emails and to Briget Harrison for going above and beyond.

Endless gratitude to Cara Conquest, Paula Gerbase and Mina Razzak for their expertise and advice.

To my friends, for their constant love, support and encouragement throughout this process, you are the MVPs and I love you; Simone Daley-Richards, Becci Hull, Vicki Davis, Sarah McCormack, Sarah Waite, Tilly Stasiuk, Lemara Lindsay-Prince, Cassandra Robinson Brown, Phy McCarthy, Thelma Badu-Yankson, Pam Omeye-Howell, Mr Ted, Sarah Mei Hughes, Tahirah Edwards Byfield, David and Madeline McQueen, Lisa Angelo-Eadie.

A big thank you to Mrs Atha's cafe in Leeds for letting me sit in there for hours while I wrote and for providing an endless supply of Earl Grey and cake.

No acknowledgement section would be complete without heaping praise upon my dog, Biggie Smalls, for providing comic relief and cuddles when the going got tough.

And lastly, to my Boom Cycle family; Rob and Hilary, thank you for being so supportive in every aspect of my career that has led me to this point. I lucked out the day I met you guys. To the incredible instructors, team and riders I'm surrounded by daily, you have kept me going, provided endless inspiration and been the very definition of cheerleaders. Thank you for believing in me. I will cheer for you always.

A note about the author

Bangs started her blog *Bangs and a Bun* in a cold bedroom in Canada in the winter of 2007. After making the decision to get active, she blogged about her journey, and before long she was the go-to girl online for all things fitness-related. In 2015, she began a two-year stint as Fitness Editor at ELLE Magazine. She lives in London, where she is the Head Instructor and Master Trainer at a boutique spin studio, making it her mission to motivate and inspire people to stay active every day.

Unbound is the world's first crowdfunding publisher, established in 2011.

We believe that wonderful things can happen when you clear a path for people who share a passion. That's why we've built a platform that brings together readers and authors to crowdfund books they believe in – and give fresh ideas that don't fit the traditional mould the chance they deserve.

This book is in your hands because readers made it possible. Everyone who pledged their support is listed below. Join them by visiting unbound.com and supporting a book today.

Rahma Adam
Collyn Ahart
Christina Albe
Emily Albou
Zeba Ali
Michelle Allen Davey
Jen Allison
Amy and the twins
Katie Andrews
Lisa Angelo-Eadie
Emese Antal
Jennifer Are
Robin Arzon
Genevieve Ascencio Alcinay
Katy Atkinson
Naomi Austin
Paul Austin
Efe Avan-Nomayo
Danny Avital
Paul Bains
Harriet Balsom

Nicola Bannock
Laura Barker
Katy Barnes
Maddie Barton
Victoria Bell
Marie Bergin
Sarah Bickley
Katie Bish
Jessica Blaikie
Jared Boetes
Ed Bonilla Jr
Ellie Box
Gemma Brady
Carla Bredin
Adrian Briggs
Sarah Broadbent-Spence
Charlotte Brown
Erin Brown
Rachel Brown
Tessa Brown
Michael Bryan

Miri Buac
Liina Buckingham
Rebecca Bull
Charlotte Bunn
Sue Burnett
Amber Burns
Fred Butler
Becca Caddy
Brendan Campbell
Brian Campbell
Jack Campbell
Ken Campbell
Peter and Jackie Campbell
Ruby Campbell
Miguel Candelario
Laura Capehorn
Armando Cardenas
Biggie Smalls Carey-Campbell
Victoria Cargill-James
Ann Carrier
Hannah Carter
Sally Carter
Isabella Castellano
Pav Chahal
Pippa Chapman
Janine Chidlow
Anita Clarke
Eleanor Clarke
Erin Clemens
Michelle Cleveland
Charli Cohen
Emma Coleman
Samantha Collier
Fiona Collin
Hannah Colton
Karyna Conder
Cara Conquest
Cat Cookman
Charlotte Cooper
Amanda Coughlin
Ruth Crawford
Claire Cripps
Fiona Cuff

Leyla Daley
Tim Dalgarno
Kelly Daniel
Nia Davies
Vicki Davis
Ísa Davvebiegga
Emma de Vries
Ruth Deane
Hannah Dell
Dewbien
Anneloes Dijkman
Adam Dikko
Melissa Doldron
Fi Donovan
Lisa Doole
Alexandra Doonan
Nicole Edwards
Tahirah Edwards-Byfield
Lauren Elizabeth
Alexis Ellison
Mark Ellison
Fiona England
Lucy Espley
Evabelle
Laura Evans
Hannah Ewart
Kate Farrell
Nina Farris
Danielle Fejer
Tanisha Ffolkes
Francina Finbow
Travis Fish
Jess Fisher
Sarah Fisher
Delali Foli
Maria Gallo
Megan Gannon
Katie Gardner
Makeba Garraway
Jennifer Garrick
Nicola Geismar
Nicola Gibb
Jo Gifford

Duncan Gilliard-Burden
Juliet Good
Jack Greaves
Sophie Green
Sabrina Greenberg-James
Laura Greene
Helen Greenwood
Rachael Gregory
Niki Groom
Steph Hamill
Emily Harrington
Erin Harris
Briget Harrison
Jane Harwood
Steph Hay
Mags HC
Jill Heilbron
Melissa Heywood-Fisher
Leyla Hobart
Kathi Hoffmann
Elizabeth Holdsworth
Amy Horton
Louise Howarth
Katherine Hudson
Michelle Huggins
Rebecca Hull
Sarah Iacovou
Elle Jackson
Lucy Jacques
Laureen Jacquet
Toto James
Rani Jassar
Lisa Jenkins
Yancy Jensen
Jessica
  @BoomCycle Hammersmith
Debbie Johnson
Emily Johnson
Esmé Johnson
Alexandra Jones
Cat Jones
Warren Jones
Zena Kamgaing

Jas Kaur
Shanti Kelemen
Dawn Rose Kelly
Jean Kemp
Lauren Kettle
Tina Khanna
Dan Kieran
Andrea Klettner
Steve Korchinos
Agnes Kowal
Heather Kuta
Pierre L'Allier
Katherine Lacey
My-Ha Lang
Jen Law
Joanne Lawen
Emma Less
Carly Lewis
Lemara Lindsay-Prince
Samantha Ling
Kerry Lister
L K Lo Dico
Christine Lobley
Julie Logan
Tarjau Louis
Louise Lowery
Melody Lubin
Nan Luma
Nick Lyell
Kimberly Lyn
Ros Lyon
Paul Lyttle
Iona MacKay Bulger
Jessie Madrigal
Heba Malik
Nicky Mamouney
Mirka Markkula
Michaela Marks
Anjali Marok
Venetia Marriott
Karen Marston
Clare Martin
Sandra Martin

Camilla Mason
Phil Mason
Isabel Massey
Fiona McCabe
Stephen McCann
Phy McCarthy
Sarah McCormack
Christina McDermott
Val McDonald
Fleur McGerr
Cat McGinty
Michelle McLean
Graham McNicholl
Bairbre Meade
Sarah Mei
Nicola Melly
Cat Mercer
Julie Meredith
John Michael Di Spirito
John Mitchinson
Jasmine Morris
Alice Morrissey
Jonathan Moss
Angela Muddle
Sarah Muluta
Holly Murray
Hannah Nathanson
Annie Naumann
Carlo Navato
Jessica Necchi
Janice Newman
Kim Ngo
Aoife Ni Chofaigh
Sarah Njie
Izzy Nkiessu-Guifo
Erin Northey
Danielle Nott
Karl Nova
Kevin O'Connor
Erinn O'Sullivan
Ronke Oke
Frances OLeary
Janet Oliver

Jess Oliver
Pamela Omeye-Howell
Ingrid Omli
Emily Oram
Orsi
Sarah Owen
Scott Pack
Khari Parson
Mihaela Pasculescu
Sheena Pattni
Katherine Pearce
Claire Pepper
Nicole Perks
Amanda Perry
Duncan Pflaeger
Catherine Pickersgill
Kelly Pietrangeli
Angharad Planells
Catherine Pollard
Justin Pollard
Lizzy Pollott
Emma Pond
Jennie Potts
Karen Preene
Kate Preston
Emma Pringle
Kellyann Prior
Alice-May Purkiss
Ali Pyner
Amy R
Reena Rai
Sarah Rathburn
Mina Razzak
Elspeth Reay
Abigail Reeve
Simone Richards
Christine Richardson
Shawna Roberts
Cassandra Robinson-Brown
Steve Ronksley
Faith Rose
Lucy Rowe
Hilary and Robert Rowland

Kate Rowlands
Zoe Rozansky
Tom S
Laura Sammarco
Karleen San Jose
Mavis Sarfo
Kate Sarginson
Yasmine Say
Angharad Saynor
Sebastian Schleussner
Lisa Serrant
Cate Sevilla
Anna Shabalova
Lindsay Sharp
Nicola Shubrook
Eva Sindelarova
Louise Sivey
Dagma Skiba
SlitCutSlash
Joanne Smalley
Toni Smerdon
Lauren Smith
Yasmin Smith
Katy Snell
Richard Soundy
Rhiannon Sowerbutts
Liesa Stecher
Ruby Steel
Alexandra Stephenson
Sara Stevanovic
Melanie Stevenson
Casie Stewart
Ben Stott
Katie Stowell
Emma Streets
Taryn Strong
Esther Summermatter
Benjamin Swanton
Hannah Swerling
Elizabeth Tait
Katy Talbot
Nic Tam
Neesha Taneja

Angie Tanner
Chloe Taylor
Ruby Teehan
Diana Teresita
Ade Thomas
Harriet Thomas
Emma Thompson
Sian Thompson
Claire Thomson
Cesar Torres
Lucy Trendle
Sophia Trim
Emma Trotter
Geraldine Tuck
Emma Turner
Charlene Valencia
Alexina Vallint-Riggs
Vishal Vashisht
Sarah Waite
Lauren Wards
Wande Wayo
Melissa Webb
Adele White
Faye White
Gemma White
Sharon White
Mark Whitfield
Corey Whiting
Dave Whittle
Laura Wickstead
Greg Wiles
Lucy Wilkins
Danny Williams
Derek Wilson
Aby Wojcik
Natalie Wood
Lucy Wright
J Wu
Irene Xanthaki
Ferida Yakubu
Roo Yeshpaul Johnson
Denis Yong
Jessie Zapotechne